WHO WHAT WHEN WHERE WHY WHO WHAT WHEN WHERE WHY WHI

THE *Pleasure* OF YOUR COMPANY

THE *Pleasure* OF YOUR COMPANY

Entertaining in High Style

KIMBERLY SCHLEGEL

WITH COURTNEY DRESLIN

PHOTOGRAPHS BY MALI AZIMA & STEPHEN KARLISCH

Gibbs Smith, Publisher

Salt Lake City

TO MY LOVING PARENTS, WHO TAUGHT ME THE VALUE OF HARD
WORK BUT ALSO THE IMPORTANCE OF HAVING FUN.

First Edition
08 07 06 05 04   5 4 3 2 1

Text © 2004 Kimberly Schlegel
Photos by Mali Azima © 2003 pages: 36–53, 114-141, 148–151, 162–171, 178–181, 188–191
Photos by Mali Azima and Mary Hilliard © 2003 pages: 172–177
Photos by Stephen Karlisch © 2003 pages: 22–35, 54–113, 152–161
Photos by Kristina Bowman © 2003 pages: 142–147
Photos by Robert Bruno © 2003 pages: 182–191

Published by
Gibbs Smith, Publisher
P.O. Box 667
Layton, Utah 84041

Orders: (1-800) 748-5439
www.gibbs-smith.com

Designed by Dawn DeVries Sokol
Printed and bound in Hong Kong

Library of Congress Cataloging-in-Publication Data
Schlegel, Kimberly.
  The pleasure of your company : entertaining in high style / by Kimberly Schlegel with Courtney Dreslin ;
photographs by Mali Azima and Stephen Karlisch.—1st ed.
     p. cm.
  ISBN 1-58685-314-7
  1. Entertaining—United States—Handbooks, manuals, etc. I. Dreslin, Courtney. II. Title.
GV1472.3.U6S35 2004
395'.3—dc22
                                    2004005057

CONTENTS

THE ART & PLEASURE
OF ENTERTAINING

ENTERTAINING plays an important role in life, one that is universal to all types of people in every segment of society. No matter how small or large the gathering, entertaining provides us with invaluable moments, the sharing of our time with family, friends, and colleagues. It provides an avenue through which memories are recollected, ideas are exchanged, new relationships ignited, and business alliances formed. You never know what may transpire. When we take the time to enjoy the pleasure of each other's company, the possibilities are endless.

One of the best things to emerge from worrisome times is the renewed appreciation most people feel for time spent with loved ones. With this shift in attitude, parties have taken on a new significance. More people are realizing that these sparkling moments in life—the ones we make time for between clocking in at the office and driving carpools—are the ones that ultimately will matter the most, the ones we will hold in our memories and reflect on with a smile.

While lavish entertaining can certainly engender lavish expenses, the only must-haves are an open mind and a creative spirit. As you will see in the examples in this book, some parties are achieved with massive budgets while others are accomplished on shoestring budgets with massive creativity.

We should never avoid entertaining in hard times, whether the culprit is a dwindling stock market or simply the winter blues. It is at these times that entertaining is most important. Festive gatherings lift our spirits by providing escapism and rescuing us from the same old routine. Every great hostess can find a good reason to slip on her favorite pair of stilettos, gather an entourage, and celebrate.

This book provides ideas, inspirations, how-tos, and tips from hosts and hostesses who regularly take time to make a difference and who add new dimensions to the art of entertaining through their distinctive personal styles. From their enormous wealth of collective talent, I have selected some of their best pearls of wisdom to share in this book. I also drew from my own

professional experience and family history in the field to include more gems of useful advice for creating magnificent events that no invited guest would dare miss.

HOW TO BE A GREAT HOST

I was fortunate to grow up in a home filled with hospitality. My parents love to entertain on all scales, and no matter what the event, they taught me that the key to successful entertaining is thoughtfulness and attention to detail. Whether they are entertaining hundreds or just having neighbors over for dinner, my mother takes the time to consider what will make the event a truly special occasion, and then meticulously prepares all the details in advance, ensuring that her guests always have a memorable experience.

My parents' philosophies and techniques greatly influence my own entertaining style, as well as my work as an event planner at my company, RSVP Soiree, where I help design all the details of my clients' special events—from the invitations to the party rentals. The fact is, with the right amount of thought and preparation, any hostess can turn that perfect party that she envisions into a reality. Although every great hostess has her own personality and signature style, what they all have in common is abiding by a few basic principles:

Above all, avoid stress

To give yourself the best chance of being a stress-free hostess, do everything in advance of party day that can reasonably be done. In other words, don't leave anything till the last day that can be done ahead. And since you're likely to be standing on your feet for several hours during the party, take a last few minutes before party guests arrive to put your feet up and relax.

Entertaining should be enjoyable for the guests *and* the host. Although the goal of entertaining is that the guests enjoy the event, this requires that you, as host, enjoy yourself as

7

well. If you appear stressed, your guests will feel guilty and uncomfortable. So even though you've worked hard and probably averted some near disasters, always make it look like there was nothing to it. In other words, you have a starring role as quintessential host, so be sure to act the part.

Just as in all areas of life, when entertaining, you cannot control everything. In order to avoid becoming a basket case anytime a mishap occurs, you must accept that anything may come your way. You never know when uninvited extras will turn up at a seated dinner, or when your electricity may suddenly go out. Later in this book, hostess Kelly Green tells the story of how she carried on even after a tornado suddenly struck her outdoor party. The best hosts have the ability to go with the flow. When faced with the unexpected, be creative and embrace change.

Preparation

Different social seasons—the most popular times of year to entertain—exist at different destinations across the country. For example, entertaining slows down in New York City come Memorial Day, at which point the parties pick up and move to the Hamptons for three cocktail-filled summer months. Do some research. If need be, check the dates that the venue and the caterer you plan to use are available. Find out when other events are scheduled, then pick a date when most

of your guests will be able to attend.

Make sure to pick a date that gives you adequate time to prepare. This includes not only the elements of your event (which I will soon discuss in detail), but also your own personal preparation time. Give yourself time to relax beforehand. You might schedule time at the spa or just get in a long walk. Don't forget to plan any beauty appointments way in advance in order to get the ideal times. Choose and try on your outfit and accessories before the day of the event and make sure any alterations or dry cleaning are taken care of in plenty of time. When you know you're looking your best, you can accomplish anything.

Make guests feel welcome

Every aspect of a party should make the guests feel comfortable. As Maria Ignez Barbosa, Ambassadress of Brazil, points out in this book, invitations should be specific and give guests enough details so they know what to expect. Guests will feel much more relaxed if they know what to wear, whether to expect cocktails and hors d'oeuvres or a seated dinner, and what the general spirit of the event will be.

The first impression is important, so greet your guests at the entrance with a smile. Try to introduce guests to others as they arrive. Keep an eye on the seating and flow of the party—these are essential to promote interaction and ensure that everyone feels included. Your most important responsibility is to make every guest feel welcome and comfortable in the setting of your party.

Details, details, details

In event planning, attending to the details is what really makes a five-star experience. It is a display of thoughtfulness by the host that makes the guests feel appreciated.

When you are celebrating a special guest, as my mother was with her luncheon for Princess Michael of Kent, the event should incorporate the personality of the guest of honor. One of the many well-thought-out details of that event were the decorations made of the breed of roses named after the Princess that my mother had flown in from England. Another fantastic example: when throwing an engagement shower for her sister, Katherine Mathes chose to serve specialty martinis named after the bride and groom (their real-life favorites).

Attention to detail applies to all events, whether you are hosting an intimate dinner party or a theme party for hundreds. The best events are those in which theme, or tone, is successfully carried out from the invitation to the décor, flowers, cuisine, music and entertainment, party favors, and even the guest book. This book is full of endless examples of how hosts and hostesses added magic to their events by mastering the details.

HIRING A PARTY PLANNER

There are times when you may not want to shoulder all of the responsibility of orchestrating an event. In these situations, event planners can be a saving grace in the planning of some or all of the elements of your event.

If you decide to hire an event planner, it is important to find one you can have confidence in. Always get references, and check with your friends for their recommendations. Interview the planners and ask many questions. What do they do especially well? Which event do they consider their crowning achievement and why? Inquire as to what vendors they work with, and check those out as well.

Once you have chosen an event planner, be sure to establish the parameters of the relationship at the beginning: what your budget is, how much personal involvement you want in the process, what you consider the most important aspects of the event. Communicate your vision for the entire event clearly. If you don't explain in detail your desired result, the planner will never be able to achieve it. If the planner is only taking care of a few specific aspects of the event, make sure they know all the other plans, as well, so they can collaborate effectively.

Attention to detail applies to all events . . .

Deciding What Type of Party to Host

There are four basic types of parties, and each type can be simple or extravagant. Here are some tips that might help you choose the one that feels right for you for the purpose or celebration you have in mind.

The Cocktail Party or Mingler
The Elements:

Guest list. Create a guest list that includes a diverse group of people who like to socialize. A cocktail party can be intimidating for a bashful friend who may be more comfortable at a structured event like a seated dinner. Cocktail parties are best when you, as the host, make the rounds and introduce people.

Drinks and hors d'oeuvres. Serve your favorite hors d'oeuvres or make them theme appropriate. It is best to have hired servers passing your selections among your guests. Decide in advance whether you will offer a full bar or a specific selection of wine, beer, specialty drinks, etc. Always offer nonalcoholic options.

Music. Music is essential to any type of event, even if you are just having friends over for a glass of wine. With the technical innovations available these days, there are many easy and inexpensive options. Software programs allow you to download songs from the Internet and play them through your stereo system. Or buy compilation CDs such as Buddha Bar or Chill brands. Just remember that cocktail party music should set the mood, not provide entertainment; so be sure it's not too loud. You want to promote conversation, not drown it out with blaring tunes. Choose music that reflects the vibe you want for the party, whether it's energetic, retro, sexy, or classical.

Special Touches:

Special-recipe drinks. Set out all of the ingredients for a specific drink on one table and display the recipe in a frame or write it in chalk on a slate. Allow your guests to experiment and have fun making their own drinks.

Taxis or car service. When hosting any party where alcohol is on the menu, line up a taxi or car service in advance for any guest who may become over-served. In addition to being safety conscious, this provides guests a discreet getaway and avoids potentially embarrassing situations.

Extra staff. Depending on the size of your event, it may be beneficial to have extra staff on hand to take drink orders and pick up or refresh empty glasses. This is a nice alternative or addition to the bar. To ensure that you won't have a kitchen full of dirty dishes waiting for you at the end of the event, consider hiring help for the cleanup.

The Basic Buffet
THE ELEMENTS:

The buffet. For buffet-style soirees, make sure to offer a sufficient amount of food selections and portions that guests feel like they have enjoyed a full meal—and that might mean going back for seconds (or thirds!). Try to set out small containers of food and replenish them often. Large containers tend to look messy and may cool off or loose their chill quickly.

Seating or cocktail tables. Make sure that your guests have plenty of space to set down their plates and drinks while they eat. Renting cocktail tables for this purpose or providing set tables gives guests a comfortable place to enjoy the cuisine.

Flow. Plan the traffic flow of your event carefully so guests will not all congregate in just one area, such as near the food or bar.

SPECIAL TOUCHES:

Theme. Be creative with your buffet and incorporate the elements of your event's theme. This adds flair to your party and gives it consistency.

Service staff. Guests rarely know what to do with their plates and glasses after they eat. Providing a service staff makes the host's job much easier and keeps the event looking good. It is often well worth the expense.

Specialty bar. Create an extensive coffee bar at your party with traditional and exotic selections. This will serve as a unique conversation piece and will prevent guests from getting sleepy.

TIP: A dessert party is a great way to entertain on a limited budget. Put on your chef's hat and create a homemade buffet of assorted sweets. Or visit your favorite bakery and order cakes, cookies, pies, cupcakes, etc. Ice cream sundae bars are always a hit. Serve hot chocolate and coffee as well.

The Memorable Meal
THE ELEMENTS:

Venue—home vs. away. Restaurants, country clubs, and hotels may offer fine menus for dinner parties, but they sometimes make it difficult to create an intimate atmosphere. Your home may be the perfect place to do the entertaining: you are comfortable with the surroundings and can control all the elements of the event. If you aren't a domestic goddess or simply don't want the responsibility of doing the cooking, you can always bring in a caterer.

Guest list. This is the most crucial aspect of a dinner party. The conversation *is* the entertainment, so make sure you assemble a lively and interesting group. Also, spend time designing the most desirable seating arrangement. Remember, as Maria Ignez Barbosa explains on page 58, the placement of people has the potential to change their lives.

The meal. Once your guests have accepted your invitation, if appropriate, you might ask if they have any food allergies. Then, no matter what courses you choose to serve, they should consist of hearty portions. Leave the small "artistic" dishes to the trendy restaurants. You don't want guests to feel like they need to go through the drive-through on their way home!

Music. When you want to give your guests something out of the ordinary, hire a harpist or piano player, carolers, a lounge singer, or string quartet. You might contact your local university or music school to find an experienced student who can perform at your event. If you do choose to hire a musician, make sure to discuss ahead of time the amount of time they will perform, the types of music you want and those that you'd like to avoid, and when they should take breaks. It is appreciated, but not required, that you provide food and drink for the musicians during their break.

SPECIAL TOUCHES:

Décor. Even if you chose a venue away from home, you can still bring your own decorations for the table. Bring something extra to match your party's theme or just enhance the environment with flowers and candles.

Place cards. Place cards have an important function, and they are also a great opportunity for you to be artistic. They can be literally any-thing—leaves, seashells, photographs. Nieman Marcus's Ken Downing (see pages 111–12) uses monogrammed trinkets, such as frames or note-books, which double as personalized party favors. Place cards do not have to be above the plates, either; they can be on the napkin rings, on the backs of the chairs, on chair pillows, etc.

Menu cards. Guests always appreciate knowing exactly what they are eating and drinking. Menu cards can also serve to formal-ize an event with traditional designs or make it more relaxed by displaying a playful one. Use your imagination: you might use recipe cards, draw a caricature of each guest, or print a fact about each guest around the card's border.

TIP: To make sure everyone feels included in the conversation, pick a topic or print a question on the place cards and have each per-son contribute their thoughts to the group. You will see one way of doing this as you read about my Peppermint Party on page 126.

TIP: When hosting large dinner parties, have some of your guests switch seats for dessert so that everyone gets a chance to visit with a variety of people.

Glamorous Gala
THE ELEMENTS:

Event planner. When entertaining on a large and lavish scale, by all means—hire help! No one can orchestrate an event of this magnitude on his or her own. As the host, part of your role at the event is to socialize and enjoy yourself. You might worry about the details in the time leading up to the event, but during the party leave it to the professionals. It's a party, after all.

Theme. A distinct theme is essential for an event of this size so it does not seem unorganized and mismatched. Choose your theme at the beginning and let it guide all of your decisions.

Entertainment. Events of this magnitude require special entertainment. A live band—if you choose a good one—can make the party. You might even hire more than one band so they can alternate sets. I prefer to have a band without vocals perform during a seated dinner and then bring out a lively cover band for post-dinner dancing. Inevitably, the band will break just when guests are getting warmed up on the dance floor, so you might have a DJ fill in during the band's down time to keep the momentum going. For those with bigger budgets, celebrity singers and musicians are fantastic selling points for fund-raisers (as at the Barnstable Brown Kentucky Derby party [page 114]) or can be exciting surprises for your guests (as you'll see at the birthday parties for Jerry Jones [page 142] and Liz Smith [page 172].) Watch out—contracts with high-profile performers can be complicated and full of odd requests! Make sure everything is clearly spelled out in the agreement.

Décor / lighting. Because you need a large venue for a gala, make it your own through décor. Fill the space in a way that will dazzle your guests. Lighting is essential to carry out the mood. Never assume that your venue will provide appropriate lighting. You may need to hire a professional lighting designer to help create the perfect atmosphere. And remember, if you want guests to dance the night away—the darker the better.

SPECIAL TOUCHES:

Valet parking. Parking is the guest's first experience at the event, so make it hassle-free.

Favors. Give your guests a memento that will remind them of the special time they spent with you. As you will see, Gene Jones makes a habit of sending framed photos from the event to her guests, and at her husband's sixtieth birthday party (page 142), she also had valet parkers place souvenir compact discs in the guests' cars.

Breakfast buffet. If your event will spill over into the after-midnight hours, change the dinner buffet to a breakfast buffet around 1 a.m. Everyone loves pancakes and scrambled eggs, and eating will refuel your guests for hours more of dancing.

TIP: When hosting a formal affair at a venue such as a restaurant or hotel, be sure to inquire specifically about the length of linens that will be used on the tables. Many venues do not provide floor-length unless requested to do so.

Fill the space in a way that will dazzle your guests.

TIP: Pay attention to the event's traffic flow. The bar will likely be the most populated area, so pick the appropriate places to keep crowds away from places where you need easy movement of people. It is a good idea to have more than one bar. You might also hire additional servers to take orders and pass drinks on trays to cut down on lines at the bar.

WINDING DOWN— THE MORNING AFTER

Don't schedule a hectic day for yourself the day after your event. Sleep late, get some R & R—you deserve it! Forget about what went wrong; things always do. Focus on what went right. Enjoy one of the best parts of entertaining: get on the phone with your friends and relive the fun. Then start planning your next party!

POSSIBLE OCCASIONS TO HOST A PARTY

Remember that every day is worth celebrating, but here are a few good excuses:
Unbirthdays/half birthdays
January blues
Tea time—formal English, or Japanese
Ladies luncheon
Pet's birthday
Groundhog day
Mardi Gras/Fat Tuesday
Valentine's singles party
Oscars (awards shows)
Bastille Day
Anniversaries
Christmas in July
Super Bowl (sporting events)
Graduation
Bon voyage
Showers—baby, wedding, housewarming
Bachelor and bachelorette parties
Book release, such as *Harry Potter* for kids
VIP visit
Poker or board game night
Retirement/promotion
Girl Scout get together complete with *the* cookies

THEME IDEAS

Geographical—French, Italian, Asian

Time periods—Victorian, Renaissance, Modern, Classical Greek, Fifties

Fairy tales—*Alice In Wonderland, Hansel and Gretel, Snow White, Rapunzel*

Literature—*The Great Gatsby, Romeo and Juliet*

Petting zoo—for kids' parties

Circus parties—for kids or adults

Seasons—summer sun, winter wonderland, harvest (see Kathryn Hall's harvest party, page 182)

Budget options—eggnog party, champagne toast, dessert buffet

TIP: When having a holiday party, don't be like everyone else. Pick a specific theme, such as a Victorian Christmas, Christmas through the decades (decorate each room of the house in the spirit of a different decade), or a peppermint party (see page 126 for my own version).

TIP: You are never too old to have a pajama party! Invite girlfriends over for treats in their slippers. You might give monogrammed pillows as favors that guests will also use at the party. Hand out slippers or comfy socks at the door. Rent chick flicks, and serve popcorn, milk and cookies. You might have a manicure/pedicure service provided. So many girlie things make perfect party favors: bubble bath, lip gloss, nail polish, etc.

HOSTESS CHECKLIST AT A GLANCE

- choose date
- choose venue
- make to-do lists—get organized early
- create guest list and collect addresses
- send out save-the-date cards as soon as you know the date of the event, and especially when out-of-town guests are involved. You may want to include information about lodging, restaurants, and local activities if you have many guests traveling to an unfamiliar destination.
- order invitations
- research potential entertainment selections
- book entertainment
- plan the menu
- select wine and other liquors
- select flowers and order from the florist
- send invitations
- check and count your serving pieces, linens, glassware, china, and silver to be sure you have everything you need
- order any necessary rentals, such as tables, chairs, and tents
- book extra services (valet parking, caterer, serving staff and cleaning service, photographer, security, coat check)
- choose any necessary place cards, menu cards, and party favors

- clear your refrigerator for your caterer; he or she will need a clean counter and as much work space as possible
- do a walk-through of your home or venue (include any staff that you have hired) to make sure each room is ready, including the powder rooms
- give yourself time to primp

A Hostess Time Table

First Thing:

Get organized. Your party planning should start by figuring out how you will keep your event organized (in a binder, a notebook, a file box, for example) and then starting to make your lists, including your time line. Be consistent with the way you organize the planning of your events. It will make future planning so much easier as you develop your own formula and then add new inspirations. Preparing in advance is a must to avoid feeling stress as your party approaches.

As Early As Possible (at the very least, one month ahead):

Choose your date. Check your local social calendars for conflicts and list your event on the calendar as well. In Dallas, the social calendar is online at *www.rsvpcalendar.com.*

Select and reserve your venue. Once you know what type of party you would like to have—cock-

tails, buffet, seated dinner—and how many guests you would like to include, you can select the appropriate venue. Maybe the theme you have chosen will affect your choice or maybe your theme will be inspired by the venue you select. Either way, keep in mind that the atmosphere of your venue will make or break your event, so choose wisely. If you decide on a location outside of the home, be sure to ask lots of questions up front. Each event venue has a different set of rules regarding all aspects of entertaining, from preferred or exclusive vendors to strict policies on set-up and tear-down. Be sure you understand all of these and that they are clearly spelled out for you before you sign a contract.

Make your guest list. Be sure to organize your guest list early and include telephone numbers for easier access later on. Leave room on the list to collect your responses as well.

Order invitations, save-the-date and pour memoir cards. You may choose to design a special custom invitation or, if you entertain often, you can order an "entertaining stationery wardrobe." This should include fill-in invitations, pour memoir cards, corresponding place cards, menu cards, and thank-you notes. Embellish with a monogram or family crest in the center or upper left corner. Save-the-date cards should be custom printed for each event and sent out as early as possible, especially if you are including guests from out of town.

Include in the first mailing information on accommodations and transportation.

FORMAL INVITATION:
FORMAL INVITATION:

Miss Kimberly Schlegel
Requests the pleasure of
(fill in guest's name)
Company at (dinner, lunch, etc.)
On (fill in date)
At (fill in time) o'clock
RSVP   Address

POUR MEMOIR (OR TO REMIND):

<u>*Pour Memoir*</u>

Mrs. Robert Schlegel
is expecting
(fill in guest's name)
for (lunch, dinner, etc.)
on (fill in date) at (fill in time)
Address

SAVE THE DATE:

Mr. and Mrs. Robert Schlegel
request the pleasure of your company
to celebrate the anniversary of their marriage.

Kindly save the date
Saturday, the thirtieth of September
Two thousand and five.

Invitation will follow

Five Weeks in Advance:

Address invitations. Invitations should always be addressed by hand, either by a professional calligrapher or someone with a beautiful natural script. As professional calligraphers usually charge by the envelope, check your list twice to confirm that you are sending the correct information to them. Many calligraphers will use their students to help address, so be sure to specify to them exactly who you would like to do your invitations.

Hire caterer and staffing and plan the menu. Word of mouth is the best way to find the caterer that is perfect for your event. If it is the first time that you are working with your caterer, ask for a tasting night where you and your committee or special friends can taste their suggestions and make your selections. Include wine and other beverages in your tasting. If you have favorite recipes, don't hesitate to share them with your caterer. Discuss staffing with your caterer early on so they can make preparations to provide you with the staff you need.

Select the wine and beverages. Once you have decided on the menu, you can select the wine and beverages that will complement your selections. If you do not feel confident making these decisions on your own, consult with the professionals at your local wine shop. Share your menu with them and ask for their suggestions to complement

Word of mouth is the best way to find the caterer . . .

17

what you have chosen. It is also important to decide whether you will provide a full bar or select cocktails, red and/or white wine, etc. As this decision will impact your list of barware needs, it is important to make it early. Ask your caterer or service staff to refrain from corking (opening) all of the bottles of your beverages at the beginning of the event. You should purchase more than you will need so you do not run out, and you will want to be able to save the remaining bottles for your next event.

Three or Four Weeks in Advance:

Mail out invitations. Double check that your addresses are correct and your list is complete, then send out your invitations. If you are including an RSVP card to be mailed back to you, be sure to include the postage to make it easy for your guests to return. Take one of your completed invitations to the post office to be weighed so you are sure you are using enough postage!

Arrange rentals and plan table settings. The rental company in your area can usually provide much assistance in helping you to figure out exactly what you will need for your event. In addition, ask your caterer for his or her needs. Rental companies can offer a great variety of linens, china, silver, and crystal for your tables, as well as kitchen equipment, coat racks, and extra trash cans. Be sure to schedule both a delivery time and

a pick-up time. Make sure the rental company's policy for pick-up is clearly communicated to your catering staff, as they will be directly handling the equipment. Ask about purchasing a damage waiver to cover breakage and/or loss so you are not surprised with a bill for replacement after the party. A big bonus: your rentals will arrive clean and you can return them dirty!

Select music and/or entertainment. Read your contracts with your entertainment very carefully and make arrangements for their needs right away.

Buy candles and other supplies. Be sure you are prepared in your kitchen and pantry for any emergency that might come up! See the list of things every hostess should have in her home (page 20) and shop for any of the items that you don't already own!

Two Weeks Ahead:

Send reminder cards. Send pour memoir cards only to those who have responded that they will be able to attend your event.

Book time at your favorite spa. Make manicure, pedicure and hair appointments for the week before your special event. I like to book a massage for the day after the event as well.

Ten Days Ahead:

Design and print a menu card. Have your menu card printed on a card stock that complements

your table design or corresponds with your invitation. Include information about the wines that will be served with the courses and any special information about each of the recipes. The top of the card should include the date and the occasion of the event, as many people save their menu cards as mementos of the special evening.

One Week Ahead:

Call guests who have not replied. Telephone numbers you included on your original guest list come in handy at this point. It is appropriate to call any guest who has not yet replied so you can be prepared for your event. Say something like, "I have not received a reply to the dinner invitation I mailed you about three weeks ago, and while I realize you may not be able to attend, I want to make sure that the invitation or your reply didn't get misplaced. If you think you can attend, I would enjoy the pleasure of your company."

Decide what you are going to wear and TRY IT ALL ON. Be sure your ensemble is clean, pressed, and fits properly. Put together in a safe place all that you will wear, from panty hose and shoes to jewelry.

Three Days Ahead:

Start set-up. If possible, start arranging your event. Set the tables and start doing any decorating that you can.

Two Days Ahead:

Plan the seating arrangement and have place cards prepared. Draw out a diagram of the tables and use the place cards to arrange the people by setting them on your chart. If you entertain often, you might benefit from purchasing a leather diagram in the shape of your table to hold and arrange these place cards (Smythson or other leather goods companies can often customize them for you.) By using the place cards, you are sure not to leave anyone out.

One Day Ahead:

Relax with your appointments at the spa. I like to get a fresh manicure and pedicure to be sure that my hands and feet are looking their best! Avoid facials or anything that might make your skin blotchy, swollen, or red!

Four Hours Before:

Do a walk-through with your staff. Walk around your entire event with your caterer and/or event planner to be sure that everything is as you expected. Delegate any last-minute duties for the event.

Two Hours Before:

Start getting ready. Leave yourself enough time to relax in the bath or take a long soothing shower before you begin your final dressing.

Half-Hour Before:

Relax. Plan to be ready for your guests to arrive at least a half hour in advance.

Sit down and sip on a beverage as you admire the amazing setting you have put together for your guests.

What Every Hostess Should Always Have on Hand

- wine, cheese and crackers
- a journal of past parties and ideas for the future
- half a dozen extra chairs in case additional seating is necessary
- small guest soaps for individual use and hand towels
- monogrammed napkins
- powder room supplies
- candles and matches
- a list of reliable vendors to call on

Tips for Working with Vendors

Rental Company
- Ask your rental company what kind of damage waiver you may purchase. Find out if it includes items that are lost as well as broken.
- Ask your rental company about their inven-

tory suggestions, whether it is something they have in stock or something they may be able to sub-rent from another rental company (this is common practice).
- Let them know at the beginning how many guests you are expecting so you can be sure that the selections you want to order are available in the appropriate quantity.
- Rentals are not just for large events. You may want to rent china or chairs for a tiny dinner party. Rentals are returned uncleaned, so it will save you from having to clean your own tableware.

TIP: To fit more people around your table, rent Chivari chairs. They are narrow and perfect for getting the maximum use of your space.

Florist
- Establish your budget up front. Describe your ideal floral look and see if they can make it work within your budget.
- Ask for a sample arrangement so you can approve it ahead of time

Caterer
- Give your caterer your favorite recipes and let them modify or work them into the menus they create for you. This is a good way for them to learn your tastes.
- If it is your first time to use a caterer, request a tasting session.
- Make sure your caterer knows not to cork (open) all of the wines and spirits you have

purchased for the event at the onset. They should be opened a few at a time as needed.

VENUES (HOTELS, RESTAURANTS, COUNTRY CLUBS)

- Inquire as to when you can begin setting up your event and by what time you must be completely cleared out.
- If necessary, see if they have extra storage space that you can make use of.

HOW TO BE A GREAT GUEST

DO RSVP in a timely manner
DO arrive on time
DO offer to help
DO dress to the theme
DO bring a hostess gift
DO write a thank-you note

DON'T bring a hostess gift that requires immediate attention (such as a flower bouquet)
DON'T get too tipsy
DON'T be a wallflower
DON'T stay past the time the party is scheduled to end

And now for the parties. There are tips and ideas to learn from every host and hostess. I hope that visiting these grand parties inspires you to throw a bash of your own.

Rentals are not just for large events.

LOLA'S FANCY DOG PARTY

WHO: Lola Chihuahua accompanied by Kim Schlegel and Allison Hopkins

WHAT: Frolic and fun for Lola and her fancy friends

WHEN: A Sunday afternoon during the dog days of summer

WHERE: In the Fido-friendly gardens and fountains at Lola's grandparents' house in Dallas, Texas

WHY: To promote maximum tail wagging, of course!

KICKING OFF THE "DOG DAYS" of a Dallas summer, Allison Hopkins and I hosted a gathering of my Chihuahua Lola's fabulous four-legged friends (and their owners) for an afternoon of frolic and fun in the garden. Inspired by the unique bond that exists among dog owners, we gathered fifty fellow pooch lovers to celebrate that special relationship. The party also served as a thank-you to our faithful furry companions for the joy they bring into our lives. Consider it our version of a slobbery lick on the lips.

Lola loves my mother's garden,
so it was easy to choose the venue.
And, unlike traditional garden par-
ties, there are no set rules for a doggie garden
party, so we were able to be creative with the
structure. With the vast array of activities we
had in mind, and taking into consideration the
socializing that would occur with that many
canines gathered together, we kept the event
to two hours on a Sunday afternoon.

The invitation was a simple yellow card
that was printed in pink and topped off with a
pink dog treat attached with ribbon. We called
the event a "Fancy Dog Party" and instructed
our guests to bring their favorite leash.
Envelopes were appropriately addressed with
the pet's name first and the owner's second.

Since dogs were the guests of honor, everything in the garden was geared toward them:

• Artist Justine Wallaceton helped each
  canine contribute to a colorful collage of
  painted paw prints.

- In another artistic endeavor, each dog and his or her owner could have their derrieres sketched into a work of art by Krandel Lee Newton, The Original Butt Sketch Artist.
- We hired a DJ and provided him with a song list that included particular selections for the occasion, including "Whatever Lola Wants," "Who Let the Dogs Out," "You Ain't Nothin' But A Hound Dog," tunes by Little Bow Wow, and "Copacabana" (you guessed it— "Her name is Lola, she was a show dog . . . ")
- A string quartet was also in the mix.
- In addition to the many, shall we say *fancy*, activities, the French Beaucerons enjoyed a good old-fashioned Frisbee toss while the water-worshiping Labradors led the swimming festivities in the garden's fountains and pools.

The décor was done in pink—Lola's favorite color. Tables were dressed in pink tablecloths draped with pastel flowers and ribbons, and

Some of Lola's fashionable friends
donned cowboy hats, sunglasses,
and other canine couture.

Lola's fancy friends all enjoyed the
party, with the Labradors leading
the water play.

Lola chose to wear a wreath of pink roses and ribbons to match. Some of Lola's fashionable friends donned cowboy hats, sunglasses, and other canine couture.

In the middle of the garden we created a beautiful doggie buffet. On a tall table (so the owners could control treat intake) sat decorative glass containers full of dog bones, biscuits, and cookies. The selections included something for all breeds and tastes—big and little, diet and regular, and every imaginable flavor. Pink Gerber daisies floated in glass vases spread intermittently among the glass treat containers.

Next was the water bar. Glass tea jars were filled with various flavored waters, including lemon, lime, mango, rosewater, Evian, and even toilet water. Owners served their pets from jeweled dog bowls loaned by Dallas's Tails of the City. By tying balloons to giant dog bones, we made sure that guests did not overlook other tables set up in the

To avoid confusion,
the people refreshments
were served by strolling
attendants.

shade. Centerpieces on those tables were stuffed dogs decked out in rhinestone tiaras and had dog-treat jars filled with flowers.

To avoid confusion, the people refreshments were served by strolling attendants carrying trays that also included Chihuahua cheese quesadillas, bite-sized hot dogs with puff pastries at each end (making them the shape of dog bones), as well as fire hydrant- and bone-shaped almond-chicken salad tea sandwiches—all prepared by chef James Roland. Champagne, chardonnay, and non-alcoholic beverages accompanied the party fare.

Party favors included canine-shaped frosted cookies for the owners and yogurt-covered biscuits for man's best friends, complete with colorful messages that read, "Thank you for stopping by to wag your tail." All guests were in agreement—Lola wins "best of show" for this stylish soiree.

"Thank you for stopping by to wag your tail."

The Original Butt Sketch Artist created artistic souvenirs for partygoers, and the hounds created a paw-print canvas of their own.

Please join
Lola
In the Garden
for a
Fancy Dog Party
Sunday, the first of June
From three until five o'clock

4444 Valley Ridge Road

Please wear your
favorite leash!
Bark Back
(214) 739-9202

Frolicky fashion was the order of the day for the pooches as well as their humans.

31

TIPS FOR HOSTING A BONE-IFIED DOGGIE BASH

Plan all the details with a lighthearted attitude. Our four-legged friends don't like being too serious.

Invite guests of all different sizes and breeds. An eclectic group is the best kind.

Hire a doggy masseuse for exceptional pampering.

While dogs play together better than their anti-social kitty counterparts, make sure there is enough room to separate them if a barking match occurs.

Make sure it is obvious to your guests whose treats are whose. Dogs will gladly share in the human food, but vice versa should be avoided.

Water is essential for drinking and for fun.

Have clean-up supplies readily available but not prominently on display.

RECIPES FOR LOLA'S GARDEN PARTY

Adapted from Chef James Rowland

PUFF PASTRY DOG BONES
Makes 32 Bones

16 beef hot dogs, halved
2 (8 x 12-inch) puff pastries
2 cups flour
3 eggs, lightly beaten with 2 tablespoons water

Split each hot dog in half lengthwise, making a total of 32 pieces. Set aside in refrigerator.

Generously sprinkle 1 cup flour on a clean surface and flour a rolling pin. Lay one pastry sheet over the floured surface. Starting from the center of the pastry, roll it evenly to twice its original size. Make sure enough flour is used so the pastry doesn't stick to the rolling pin's surface. Brush off any excess flour from the pastry with a pastry brush or dishcloth.

Cut the now-bigger pastry lengthwise into 8 equal strips. Each strip should be just over an inch in width. Next, cut each strip into 4 equal pieces, making a total of 32 pieces. Repeat process with second pastry sheet. Use the reserved cup of flour for this step. Once you are finished you should have 64 pastry pieces.

Now, using 2 pastry pieces per hot dog section, carefully wrap each end with the seam-side down so it resembles a bone (seam should be on flat side of hot dog half). Place bone on a baking sheet that has a generous amount of cooking spray. Repeat process to make 32 bones. Space bones about 1 inch apart from each other. Using a pastry brush, paint the pastry ends with the egg wash. Place in refrigerator for 1 hour.

Preheat oven to 400 degrees. Bake for 20 minutes, or until the pastry is golden brown. Serve with yellow mustard.

Almond Chicken Tea Sandwiches
Makes 40 Sandwiches

Ingredients:

4 pounds boneless chicken breasts, chopped

2 pounds slivered almonds

⅓ cup + 1 tablespoon chives, minced

¼ cup parsley, finely chopped

¼ cup green onion, finely chopped

2 cups Mascarpone cheese, room temperature

2 cups mayonnaise

2 tablespoons lemon zest

¼ cup lemon juice

¼ cup kosher salt

2 tablespoons white pepper

4 loaves Pullman bread, white or wheat

Preheat oven to 400 degrees. Spread almonds on a baking sheet and toast for 10 minutes, or until light golden brown. Set aside for later use.

Cook chicken in a large skillet over medium-high heat until completely cooked through. You may need to do this in a few batches. Drain any excess liquid and allow to cool completely. Once cool, coarsley chop cooked chicken in a food processor

In a large mixing bowl, combine the chicken, almonds, and all remaining ingredients except bread. Combine well so all items are evenly mixed and coated. Correct the seasoning, cover, and refrigerate.

Cut the crusts off all 4 loaves of bread. Then slice each loaf into 4 lengthwise slices. Roll each slice of bread with a rolling pin to flatten slightly. Cover with a damp dish towel until used.

Spread chicken mixture evenly on 8 of the bread slices. Keep mixture more toward the center so the chicken isn't discarded with the excess bread once it is cut. Cover chicken with remaining bread slices. Wrap the 8 long sandwiches tightly in plastic wrap and refrigerate for 2 hours.

When ready to serve, place a bone-shaped cookie cutter over one side of the sandwich, and press firmly into the bread. You should be able to cut 5 cookie-cutter-sized pieces per long sandwich. It is important that the cookie cutter is cleaned after each impression to avoid sticking. Arrange sandwiches on a decorative platter and serve.

HOMEMADE DOG BISCUITS
Makes approximately 100 2-ounce biscuits

2 pounds white flour
1 pound wheat flour
1 pound cornmeal
1 pound rolled oats
½ cup liver powder
½ cup garlic powder
¼ cup onion powder
¼ cup salt
1 gallon water

Sift together all dry ingredients, then place in a 5-quart countertop mixer. Using a dough hook over medium speed, slowly add water. The dough's consistency should be very firm. Mix for 5 minutes, then remove from bowl. Let dough sit for 1 hour.

On a clean, flat surface, roll out half the dough to ½ inch thickness. Using a cookie cutter of choice, punch out the dough biscuits and place them one inch apart on a baking sheet. Roll out the excess dough again. Repeat the process until all the dough has been used.

Preheat oven to 400 degrees. Bake for 20 minutes, or until biscuits are firm to touch. The biscuits will dry out, so be careful not to cook biscuits too long. Cool and store in an airtight container or zipper-lock bag.

A NIGHT IN SEVILLE

WHO: International hostess Becca Cason Thrash and her husband, John Thrash

WHAT: A Spanish-themed extravagala starring salsa singer Marc Anthony

WHEN: Saturday noche

WHERE: Longwoods, the Thrashes' modern megamansion in Houston, Texas

WHY: To benefit Best Buddies, a nonprofit agency founded by Anthony Kennedy Shriver

ONE MIGHT SAY THAT YOU HAVEN'T TRULY been to a party until you've been to a party hosted by Becca Cason Thrash. This Houston-based fund-raiser and internationally celebrated hostess has been deemed the "high priestess of posh" and a "social cyclone." Her parties have fascinated the likes of *W*, *Harper's Bazaar*, *Town and Country*, *Talk*, *Texas Monthly*, and Liz Smith—to name just a few.

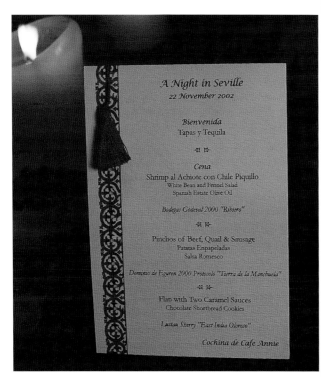

This particular gala met her usual fare for flare. It was Becca's annual benefit for Best Buddies, a nonprofit organization founded by her friend Anthony Kennedy Shriver that promotes independence and inclusion for people with intellectual disabilities. People were still talking about her previous year's "Shanghai in the Spring" Asian fantasy, when Becca delivered another dreamy night of decadence— this time "A Night in Seville."

Becca admits that her now world-famous themes began simply because she had a dramatic yellow Mandarin-collared Marc Bouwer couture gown that desperately needed an occasion. From this age-old fashionista dilemma sprung "Shanghai in the Spring."

The Spanish theme was carried through every aspect of the party, from the invitation to the food and the entertainment.

"Think lace, ruffles, flamencos, boleros . . . Be bold! Be bonita!"

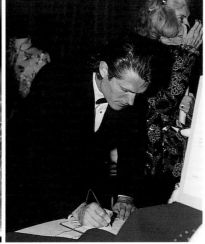

"Theme parties are more fun and more cohesive because people really get into the spirit," Becca says. She explains that it is crucial that the guests make a participatory contribution to the festivities. For example, regarding the Seville party, she quipped, "If they can't put a rose in their hair or slip on a Spanish-inspired shawl, then, in my opinion, they should stay home."

The Spanish-themed invitation featured a bullfighter and an exotic *señorita* in traditional attire, inspiring visions of what might possibly be in store. But those familiar with Becca's bashes know that one can never predict just what may be up her glamorous sleeve. Three hundred guests were invited (in English and Spanish) to the Thrashes' estate in Houston to indulge in tapas and cocktails followed by a Spanish feast and—hold onto your sombreros—a performance by Latin sensation Marc Anthony. *Ole!* The attire was presented as "high black tie, Spanish-inspired." To assist the guests in selecting the most appropriate apparel, Becca added, "Think lace, ruffles, flamencos, boleros . . . Be bold! Be *bonita!*"

Designer Richard Flowers worked with Becca to transform her 20,000-square-foot granite, slate, and glass mansion into a Spanish extravaganza. Tables were draped with black-and-gold embroidered fabric, then decorated with iron candelabra centerpieces intertwined with thousands of red roses and colorful fruits. The setting was stunning with hundreds of lighted candles, as Becca has said that she wouldn't dream of having a party without them.

Another of her favorite gala accessories are models dressed in the evening's theme. So, as if the invitation had sprung to life, bullfighters with scarlet sashes and dazzling flamenco ladies with bright red lips and red roses mingled with the guests. Red definitely seemed to be the color of the night. Becca herself wore a John Galliano red-fringed couture gown that simply dripped divine. Her guests didn't disappoint either. Everywhere you looked there were ruffles, lace, fringe, and other Spanish trimmings. Roses in all shades of sangria were in hair and on

The tapas were not only delectable but delightful to the eye.

Traditional Spanish tapas accompanied more tequila during the silent auction.

BECCA'S TIPS FOR HOSTING A THRASH-WORTHY BASH

You can kill yourself with the menu, the décor, the music; but the most important aspect is the people. Assemble a varied guest list with some outrageous guests or surprise celebrity guests, if possible. Mix it up with old people and young people, old guard and new guard, etc.

Keep the drinks coming to keep the party lively. Becca even encourages her guests to drink shots immediately upon arrival. Arrange ahead for designated drivers or safe transportation home for all.

Choose exhilarating music.

Create an intoxicating atmosphere with candles, theme décor, etc. It has been said that a house is at its very best right before guests arrive. The visual aspect of the home plays an important role in setting the scene as the guests walk in.

evening bags. There were embroidered shawls, lace gloves, and an authentic antique fan that someone had picked up in Seville. One gentleman arrived as Zorro, complete with a red cape. There was no shortage of beautiful people or of couture.

Dozens of attendants at the entrance to the affair made sure that each guest had tequila in hand on arrival, and then kept it flowing all evening long. (Becca advocates keeping the spirits flowing to keep the guests loose, and on this occasion margaritas were mixed past three

Marc Anthony, the hottest star of Latin music, to graciously donate his time in a sensational performance, thus completing her flawless Spanish apparition. So guests could enjoy the performance under the stars, a stage and dance floor were constructed on the home's lavish landscape.

in the morning.) Traditional Spanish tapas accompanied more tequila during the silent auction. The guests were then seated for three courses of Spanish fare: Shrimp al Achiote con Chile Piquillo; White Bean and Fennel Salad with Spanish Estate Olive Oil; Pinchos of Beef, Quail & Sausage with Patatas Enpapeladas and Salsa Romesco; Flan with Two Caramel Sauces; and Chocolate Shortbread Cookies. All were prepared by Houston's Café Annie and accompanied by selections of Spanish wine. Menu cards at the place settings were printed on paper that perfectly matched the embroidery of the table dressing, complete with festive red tassels.

Latin music is a must for a Spanish-themed party, and leave it to Becca to enlist

While some chose to groove to the Latin beat on the dance floor, others looked on from cocktail tables warmed by tall tree heaters and the steamy performance.

It is obvious that Becca throws parties much like the way she lives life. She often quotes Diana Vreeland, *Vogue*'s editor during the sixties, who said, "You have to have style. It's what gets you up in the morning." And, in this case, it was that unmistakable Becca style that kept guests enchanted all night long. The benefit was a huge success for Best Buddies, and the evening, in Becca's own words, was a "*noche to remember.*"

A LUNCHEON FIT FOR A PRINCESS

WHO: My mother, hostess extraordinaire Myrna Schlegel

WHAT: A luncheon in honor of Her Royal Highness Princess Michael of Kent

WHEN: A splendid spring afternoon

WHERE: The Schlegel family's French-inspired gardens and house in Dallas, Texas

WHY: To celebrate the crown jewels of life—friends and family

GREAT BRITAIN'S HER ROYAL HIGHNESS Princess Michael of Kent, in addition to being legitimately titled, is quite a scholar and the highly acclaimed author of many historical books. She occasionally travels to the United States to lecture on her latest musings, and it was during one of these trips that my mother, Myrna Schlegel, hosted a ladies' luncheon in her honor.

Experiencing Britain's royal protocol made the day especially memorable.

Menu

Mixed field greens salad with
Caramelised pecans, apple and goat cheese
Apple cider honey vinaigrette
§
Almond herb crusted chicken breast
Served over grilled vegetables
Red pepper aioli
§
Fruit Medley with orange and port reduction

I have grown up watching my mother entertain on a frequent basis, so I have had the privilege of learning from her expertise and extraordinary style. Trevor Erskine-Meade, who has served as my family's butler for years, aptly describes my mother when he explains that she "strives for perfection in all aspects of her life, including her role as hostess."

My mother often says that "entertaining is a way to celebrate great friendships." So, for the afternoon with Her Royal Highness Princess Michael of Kent, the guest list included some of my mother's closest friends. These women also form quite an eclectic and exceptional group, among whom are an art historian, an opera singer, a former ambassador to Austria, and many other women who if Dallas had its own royalty would certainly qualify.

While London still favors the level of formality required in bygone eras, such pageantry is no longer necessary or the norm in other locales. However, particular traditions and rules of etiquette always apply when

entertaining members of the royal family. After the guests received their invitations, a pour memoir was sent. In accordance with strict royal protocol, it was formally worded: "In the presence of Her Royal Highness Princess Michael of Kent, Mrs. Robert Schlegel expects you for champagne in the garden at 11:30 a.m., seated luncheon at 12:30 p.m."

The garden at the Schlegel home was at its finest that afternoon. The tables were draped in sheer blue overlays accompanied by crystal vases filled with countless blue hydrangeas. With all the garden's flowers perfectly in bloom, the surroundings looked appropriately stolen from the English countryside. Surrounded by flowing fountains, the guests sipped tea and champagne as Dallas Mayor Laura Miller presented the Princess with a key to the

The place settings were
perfectly aligned, in the same
manner that is adhered to
in England's royal ceremonies.

city. It is well known that the Princess collects such keys, and many cities have been honored to contribute to her collection.

My mother and the Princess then led the guests inside to the formal dining room for the seated luncheon. The dining room is one of the most unique rooms in my mother's home because the carved wood and painted panels were all imported from an eighteenth-century home in Paris. For this occasion, the dining room was simply stunning, set exclusively in Baccarat with delightful blue accents. The place settings were perfectly aligned, in the same manner that is adhered to in England's royal ceremonies. Hundreds of blue hydrangeas cascaded from fine crystal vases. The china was an ornate pattern edged in gold and azure. "I selected this pattern for its daytime, springy air—it is perfect for a luncheon," my mother said. "The same design is often used at Buckingham Palace and the White House." Charming crystal figurines of butterflies and birds in blue added to the room's elegant ambiance.

One of my mother's philosophies for entertaining is that every event should exhibit not only the personality of the host but the guest of

MYRNA'S ADVICE FOR ELEGANT ENTERTAINING

Always find out something special about the person you are honoring and incorporate that detail into your event.

The host and hostess should always be at the entrance to greet and later to say good-bye to their guests.

Make everyone feel included. For instance, pick a topic of conversation or question and ask each guest at the table for her opinion.

Treat every guest like royalty.

honor as well. So, in a divine display of detail, my mother had the breed of roses that are named after Her Royal Highness Princess Michael of Kent flown in from England. Each guest received one of the yellow namesake roses at her place setting in a blue Baccarat bud vase. The Princess was pleasantly surprised, as were the other guests.

There is no doubt that a British chef knows best what to serve British royalty. With this in mind, the menu was created by Chef Louise Kenhard of England, who was flown in to help prepare the selections with Dallas's Chef James Rowland. The culinary selections consisted of a mixed field greens salad with caramelized pecans, apple, and goat cheese with apple cider honey vinaigrette; almond herb-crusted chicken breast served over grilled vegetables and red pepper aioli; and a fruit medley with orange

and port reduction. In another special gesture, my mother chose the wine for this affair specifically from the vineyard of one of her guests. There were also petits fours, coffee, and tea. My grandmother, Myrtle Horst, gave the blessing, and later my mother made the customary toast to the Princess. While the guests dined and socialized, a string quartet played music.

In addition to the royal roses, gifts for the guests included clear crystal Baccarat hearts, which were arranged on a nearby table under an exquisite bouquet of Her Royal Highness Princess Michael of Kent roses. "I thought this was an appropriate gift since all of the guests were friends and family I hold close to my heart," my mother explained. "I also wanted to give my guests something that they would keep forever and that would always remind them of this day with the Princess."

RECIPES ADAPTED FROM THE PRINCESS MICHAEL OF KENT LUNCHEON

MIXED FIELD GREENS SALAD WITH CARAMELIZED PECANS, APPLES, AND GOAT CHEESE, WITH APPLE CIDER HONEY VINAIGRETTE

Makes 8 servings

To make Caramelized Pecans:

¼ cup butter

2 cups pecans

1 cup sugar

8–10 ounce log of mild goat cheese, cut into 8 equal slices

2 Granny Smith apples, cored, sliced, and quartered

Melt butter in a large frying pan, then add the pecans and sugar. Stir until light golden brown and syrupy—about 5 minutes. Pour onto a greased baking sheet to cool.

To make Apple Cider Honey Vinaigrette:

1 cup clear honey

3 tablespoons Dijon mustard

1 cup apple cider vinegar, best quality

1 cup canola oil

1 cup olive oil

Mix honey, mustard, and vinegar in a blender. Very slowly add the oils through the top while continuing to mix until thick.

To assemble the salad:

8 cups mixed field greens

Place one cup field greens in the center of each plate. Top with one slice of goat cheese, some pecans, and some of the sliced apples. Arrange decoratively. Drizzle dressing over top.

Almond and Herb-Crusted Chicken served over Grilled Vegetables with Red Pepper Aioli

Makes 8 servings

To make Red Pepper Aioli:

2 egg yolks
1 garlic clove
1 cup extra virgin olive oil
1 cup canola oil
3–6 tablespoons white balsamic vinegar
1 roasted red pepper
1 teaspoon salt

Place yolks and garlic in a blender. Slowly pour the oils through the top and blend on high speed until thick. Add the vinegar and pepper, then puree; it should be pinkish in color. Season with salt. Pour into a ketchup squeeze bottle and refrigerate.

To make herb-crusted chicken:

3 cups Japanese panko or fresh bread crumbs
1 handful of fresh mixed herbs (basil, rosemary, oregano, and thyme), to taste
4 eggs
6 tablespoons water
1 cup extra virgin olive oil, divided
8 chicken breasts, slightly flattened if uneven
Salt and pepper, to taste

Mix panko or breadcrumbs and herbs until just combined. Put on a plate.

In a wide, shallow bowl, lightly beat the eggs and water together to make egg wash.

Heat ½ cup of olive oil in a large, heavy-bottomed frying pan over medium heat.

Season each chicken breast with salt and pepper. Dip each breast into the egg wash and then into the crumb mixture. Cook 4 breasts at a time in the oil for 4–5 minutes on each side, or until golden brown. Add a little oil to the frying pan before cooking second batch. Keep chicken in a warm oven while you cook the next batch.

To roast vegetables:

2 eggplants
2 zucchinis
2 each red, yellow, and green peppers

Slice each vegetable into one-inch-thick slices. Brush each side with remaining oil and grill on a barbecue until tender and browned.

To assemble the dish:

1 handful basil, chiffonade

Fan vegetables on one side of each plate, then place chicken on the other side. Drizzle with aioli. Top with a chiffonade of basil.

MELON BERRY MÉLANGE WITH PORT WINE SYRUP
Makes 8 servings

For the syrup:
2 cups Port wine
1 cup Beaujolais or any red wine
1 cinnamon stick
4 lemon slices, each stuck with 1 clove
6 tablespoons honey
1 teaspoon salt

Fruit:
2 honey dew melons
4 cantaloupes
2 cups blackberries
2 cups raspberries
Mint for garnish

To make the Port Wine Syrup:
Combine all the ingredients in a 2-quart saucepan and bring to a boil. Allow the liquid to simmer until it has reduced by half, or until the liquid coats the back of a spoon. Pour through a fine-mesh strainer into a container and allow to cool. Refrigerate until ready to use.

To prepare the fruit:
Cross cut 2 one-inch slices out of the center of each cantaloupe (8 rings total) with skin on. Clean out the seeds, then remove outer skin with a sharp knife. Set aside.

Using a melon-baller, scoop out nice round pieces of the honey dew melon and the unused cantaloupe and place in a mixing bowl.

Gently toss the berries and melon balls with ½ cup of the Port Wine Syrup.

To serve:
Center the cantaloupe rings on 9-inch plates, then spoon the melon-berry mixture into mounds inside the melon rings. Drizzle the remaining syrup over and around the fruit. Garnish with a mint sprig and serve.

DIPLOMATIC DINNER

WHO: Maria Ignez Barbosa, Ambassadress of Brazil

WHAT: A dinner of diplomats

WHEN: At the changing of the political season

WHERE: The Brazilian Embassy Residence, Washington, D.C.

WHY: To say thank you and farewell to Brazilian diplomats ending their term

WHEN I MENTIONED TO MY FRIEND Christophe Gollut, a world-renowned interior designer, that I was publishing a book on entertaining, he said, "You simply *cannot* do such a book without including Ambassadress Maria Ignez Barbosa; she is one of the most stylish hostesses in the world." A few weeks later, when I visited the Brazilian Embassy's Residence in Washington, D.C., for one of Maria and her husband Ambassador Rubens

Maria Barbosa's philosophy is that a dinner party is an opportunity to share intellectual ideas, to grow and develop through time spent together.

Barbosa's revered dinner parties, I was instantly convinced that Christophe was quite correct.

The raison d'etre of this particular evening was to toast the diligence of the diplomats who had concluded their terms and were soon returning home to Brazil. Such dinner parties are a frequent fixture at this embassy, as they were at Maria and her husband's previous post as ambassadors in London, and before that, at their home in Brazil. Unlike most of the working world, the job responsibilities of government representatives don't cease at the end of the workday. Ambassador Barbosa, for instance, admitted that he wears a tuxedo at least twice a week. The Barbosas have hosted all sorts of dignitaries and who's-who types, including Sean Connery, supreme court justices, and most of the modern-day royals. While residing at the London Embassy, they hosted a never-to-be-forgotten dinner party for the Queen of England, ten other members of England's royal family, and members of London's aristocracy.

This sort of lifestyle is in Maria's blood. Both her mother and grandmother were ambassadresses of Brazil, and, interestingly, both served in London as well as Washington. "I remember my grandfather, who was a politician in Brazil, had the dining room table set every night, and every night people came over," she said. Her childhood memories are filled with watching her parents entertain in the same sort of social circles. But she is quick to point out that Brazilians, in general, are known for their

"Now that we are serving as ambassadors, we have to entertain within the government's budget, so I have to be creative."

hospitality. "In Brazil, even the poor are very generous people."

"We have loved receiving people since we were very young," she reminisces. "Now that we are serving as ambassadors, we have to entertain within the government's budget, so I have to be creative." Exhibits of her innovation and great style are visible throughout the residence. As she effortlessly prepared for the evening's festivities, Maria shared her wisdom and her secrets to success.

Starting with invitations, Maria advises, "be precise. You need to say if it is a seated dinner, otherwise people will just drop by." Location makes a difference. "Each city offers different types of people," she explains. For example, people in Brazil tend to eat later than the early-to-bed politicians in Washington. Also, events in our nation's capital are usually either cocktail or black-tie attire. Maria specifies this on the invitation, as well. However, she expounds, in D.C., unlike many other parts of the country, the focus is not on wardrobe but rather on the exchange of intellectual ideas.

What interests Maria most about entertaining is, simply, the guests. She delights in uniting a mixture of society—artists, politicians, historians. "You should grow and develop through your time spent together," she says. "It is nice when you leave the party and feel stimulated by the conversation. You learn more through people than you do through books."

She notes that it is important that the environment lend itself to conversation. This means paying close attention to how the rooms are set up. In large rooms where guests are to have cocktails before dinner or après-dinner drinks, she makes sure there is more than just one area of seating for people to congregate. "You want to make sure the guests are comfortable so they can relax and be themselves." This also means respecting privacy, with no photographers. (Note that for this event, there are no pictures of the guests.) As for seating arrangements for dinner, she puts great

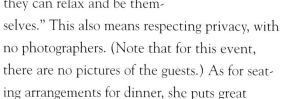

Maria advises that the entire house should be attended to with flowers and other decorative details.

thought into who sits next to whom. After all, "the placement of people can change lives," she says. And she makes sure that chairs aren't so far apart as to discourage conversation.

Maria advises that the entire house should be attended to with flowers and other decorative details, since a whole evening is not often spent in the dining room, even for dinner parties. The embassy's residence, a classic home designed by architect John Russell Pope (who also designed the National Gallery of Art, the Thomas Jefferson Memorial, and the National Archives), is already one of the most brilliant and becoming buildings on Embassy Row.

However, it is Maria's fascinating décor and personal touches that make the residence a stylish home. Every inch of space boasts something special. The framed caricature of Maria and her husband that is displayed next to their guest book debuted on the menu at their welcome dinner when they first arrived in Washington. The artist was obviously aware of the Barbosas' reputation for high style. One could browse for hours among the collection of fine paintings and modern sculpture, Venetian mirrors, art deco

vases, and photographs. Much like in a museum, everything seems to have a wonderful story behind it, but in this case the stories are Maria's.

Floral décor is another of Maria's talents. This evening, stark white calla lilies arranged in asymmetrical designs, often in front of mirrors, seemed to defy the laws of physics. Some were arranged so they stretched toward each other from tall glass vases in varying heights. In the dining room, the silver vases had three-tiered bases that gave the flowers interesting spatial aesthetics. In fact, all the arrangements themselves were works of art.

Maria always collaborates with the embassy's chef to design delicious, diverse menus. She notes that the current environment calls for lighter fare, and she makes sure that the same ingredients are not repeated in successive courses. Since she is often hosting government affairs, they try to invent international cuisine with Brazilian flair. For example, the colors of one course might display the yellow and green hues of the Brazilian flag. However, she warns that the food must be good, not just beautiful. She also uses beautiful

serving dishes and china. Some pieces are the same treasures with which her mother and grandmother entertained.

The evening that I visited with her, the first course of soup was indeed in the patriotic colors of Brazil. It was a yellow tomato soup with a creative twist—a scoop of spinach sorbet in the center.

If you keep a record of what is served at your parties and who attends, you can always offer original menus no matter how often you entertain.

The next course consisted of a gourmet crab dish accompanied by roasted vegetables. And the desserts were splendid—chocolate mousse served in unique chocolate cups along with cookies.

For those who entertain often, Maria proposes keeping a record of the menu served, who ate what, and who sat next to whom. Then you don't accidentally repeat the same scenario on the guest's next visit. For special events, Maria puts great thought into party favors. At her soiree honoring the anniversary of the Embassy, each guest took home a puzzle of the residence.

Even with all the details to tend to, Maria makes every aspect of such thoughtful, elegant entertaining look easy. But she does admit that "sometimes the organizing is more enjoyable than the party." A statement that hosts and hostesses everywhere can relate to.

DIPLOMATIC TIPS

Invitations should be precise in all respects: cocktails or meal to be served, attire expected, times to come and go.

A good mix of guests ensures a good party. Interesting people create interesting discussions, which will be the ultimate memory for guests.

Set the stage of your event to stimulate conversation and provide the comfort needed so guests can relax and be themselves. With high-profile guests, privacy must be ensured.

Make the setting beautiful and the food memorable. Color, texture, and diversity are important for both.

Keep a log of events so you'll remember the mix of invitees and the food served to avoid repetition at future events.

Soupe de Tomates Jaunes au Sorbet Depinards
Makes 8 servings

For the soup:
6 leeks, only the white part, diced
8 yellow tomatoes, diced
2 onions, diced
6 garlic cloves, crushed
1 pinch saffron

Olive oil, for sauteing
2 cups white wine
4¼ cups chicken consommé
1 Greek yogurt, nonfat
Salt and pepper, to taste

In a frying pan, saute leeks, tomatoes, onion, garlic and saffron for 10 minutes with a little olive oil. Add the wine and consommé. Cook on low for one hour. Let cool. Mix in the blender with nonfat yogurt, adding salt and pepper to taste.

For the sorbet:
2 one-pound bags spinach, cooked and pureed
4¼ cups chicken consommé
1 tablespoon sugar
1 Greek yogurt, nonfat
1 pinch salt
1 pinch white pepper

Mix all ingredients in an ice cream maker until set (about 45 minutes).
To serve, ladle soup into bowls and add a scoop of sorbet.

ENGAGEMENT CELEBRATION

WHO:	Party planner Katherine Mathes
WHAT:	An elegant engagement party
WHEN:	Saturday evening during the social season
WHERE:	A Dallas restaurant with romantic outdoor gardens
WHY:	To celebrate her sister's upcoming nuptials

KATHERINE MATHES USUALLY PLANS other people's events. She spends her professional life as a party planner with RSVP Soiree, picking perfect invitations, suggesting glamorous glassware, choosing the most apropos china, and performing incredible table makeovers. Clients also count on her to tend to the lower profile yet *trés* important details: studying the venue, calculating how many tables are needed and what size, hiring the valet. So, when she hosted a party of her own—an

Choosing a restaurant venue precludes a lot of the stress that comes with hosting a party.

mental for Katherine and her mother, who cohosted the gathering, they put great thought into the details to make it an extra special experience for everyone involved. "We really wanted the entire event to reflect the personalities of both the bride and the groom." Katherine said. From the inception through the entire planning process, she kept that goal in mind. The guests of honor had planned their wedding to take place outdoors on a picturesque mountaintop, and Katherine decided that the engagement party should preview that coming attraction. While Dallas has no mountains to speak of, the city does have glorious gardens. After considering several options, Katherine decided on Marie Gabrielle, a romantic restaurant-and-garden venue. "The destination had everything we were looking for: a gorgeous outside garden setting, a relaxed environment inside, and a great central location."

engagement party for her sister and the groom-to-be—it was an ideal opportunity to show some techniques of a bona fide expert.

Since this occasion was particularly senti-

After selecting a weekend night that was not already filled with social engagements or charitable undertakings and that would accommodate the out-of-town guests, it was time to

"It is important to give the guests guidance
so they feel comfortable when they arrive at the party."

send the invitations. "Invitations are the calling card to the event, as they set the tone and feel for the party," Katherine explains. "For this occasion, we wanted something fun, simple, and elegant." She decided on a selection from Caspari that had a pretty but understated pink border. In addition to including all the necessary information regarding the party, Katherine advises that invitations should always include the suggested attire. "It is important to give the guests guidance so they feel comfortable when they arrive at the party." After all, in our current climate of everyday casual, it's especially hard to determine when one should lose the go-anywhere jeans in favor of a cocktail dress.

Katherine explains that, typically, invitations should be sent three weeks before the event, but if out-of-town guests are in the mix, it is polite to give two month's notice in order for guests to arrange travel. Including maps for the out-of-towners is also a wise and often appreciated gesture that is likely to prevent frantic cell phone calls at the last minute.

At Marie Gabrielle, Katherine arranged for all the guests to enter via a special walkway that led through the gardens. Torches lit the way, adding ambiance but also preventing missteps in Manolos. Much to the delight of many, the path led straight to a martini bar. The bride and groom are both fond of martinis, and as you probably guessed, the choice of four flavors reflected the favorites of the guests of honor. "Be creative with the drinks," Katherine suggests. "Name a drink after the bride and one for the groom. And don't be afraid to introduce new drinks or uncommon selections—it shows originality."

And so the party began, with guests sipping martinis and enjoying passed hors d'oeuvres in the garden.

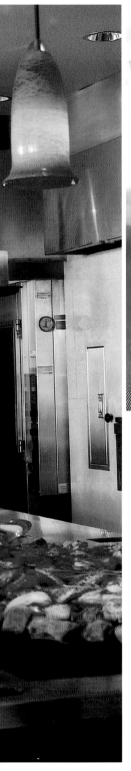

A piano player provided a repertoire of songs that hopscotched through the decades, providing guests of all ages with familiar tunes as they mingled and left their remarks in the guest book.

Inside the restaurant, Marie Gabrielle has a rustic Texas feel with dark-toned floors, iron figures, and hundreds of candles. The ceiling consists of imaginative light fixtures that resemble lovely lily pads. Katherine selected both cocktail and larger tables to best accommodate the eighty guests in this setting. For the flowers and table décor, she chose a lime green-and-chocolate color scheme, which accentuated the surroundings and reflected an outdoorsy, nature look. Two Design Group created the alluring botanical atmosphere with elaborate arrangements of assorted green flowers, plants, and fruits—all accented with chocolate hues and accompanied with tall iron candelabras. Even the glassware matched the theme; it was green-tinted glass etched in gold. Luxurious linens were rich brown in color and the elegant chair covers were sheer white with gold stitched leaf detailing. Equally enticing was the Latin music provided by a three-piece band.

The party was from 6 to 9 in the evening, which calls for more than just hors d'oeuvres. The hostesses decided on a dinner buffet. "We didn't want a seated event, and this allowed the guests to dine at their pleasure, giving them more flexibility to speak with the bride and groom, who were in

high demand." The buffet selections provided something for all tastes but focused on the bride and groom's favorite—seafood. Grilled salmon dressed with thyme and kept warm over hot rocks was the highlight, but assorted sushi, beef tenderloin, grilled vegetables and martini mashers were all thoroughly enjoyed. Martini mashers consist of everyone's favorite comfort food, mashed potatoes, with a choice of toppings such as chives, cheese, bacon, sometimes even chicken fingers—all served in a martini glass. "They are perfect for eating while standing," Katherine explains. There was also a cheese-and-fruit display that was almost too attractive to eat. Finally, a chocolate fondue fountain added flair to the dessert station—a finishing touch requested by the bride.

This intimate, personalized affair not only touched the bride and groom, but was a touching tribute to a very special upcoming event. Everyone left with anticipation for the "I do" festivities, the next chapter in this couple's happily ever after.

TIPS FOR A THOUGHTFUL ENGAGEMENT PARTY

There is a perfect venue for every event— the key is to match them correctly.

The invitation sets the mood, so put a lot of thought into your selection.

Select a menu that will cater to everyone but will especially please the guests of honor.

Be creative with the drinks. Don't be afraid to feature the unusual and name a new drink after the bride and groom.

Spice up the glassware, serving wine in a colored water glass, beer in a pilsner, or martinis in short, round high-ballers adds a fun, interesting touch.

Figure out the parking situation in advance, and make sure there is a convenient entrance for handicapped guests.

Plan ahead and be organized but don't let problems ruin the planning process or the party—there is always a suitable solution.

A BOOK BASH, HAMPTONS-STYLE

WHO: Marcy and Michael Warren,
Hillary Swank and Chad Lowe, Marty Richards

WHAT: A who-done-it book bash

WHEN: During a summer sunset

WHERE: Marcy and Michael Warren's Hamptons estate
in Water Mill

WHY: To promote page turning

MENTION THAT YOU'RE HEADING TO THE HAMPTONS in the summer, and you're sure to invoke visions of glittering parties overflowing with VIPs sipping cocktails as the sun sets over the water. And in reality, well, that's exactly how it is.

Frequent New York entertainers Marcy and Michael Warren hosted this summer shindig at their estate in Water Mill along with Oscar-winning actress Hillary Swank and her husband, Chad Lowe, and Oscar-

> "The uniqueness about entertaining in the Hamptons is that the world is your oyster."

winning producer Marty Richards. It was a book-launch party for their friend Karin Yapalater, who had just penned her first thriller, *An Hour to Kill.* The turnout was impressive, even for the Hamptons, and *Page Six* was there leading the contingent of media types who were eating up the celebrity scene along with the caviar. In addition to the star-studded collection of hosts, guests included Denise Rich, Edie Brickell Simon, Star Jones, *Saturday Night Live* producer Lorne Michaels, and author James Patterson, to name just a few.

The hosts may be a glamorous group, but they weren't afraid to roll up their sleeves a little to do all the decorating themselves. Karin set the stylish cocktail tables with sunny yellow tablecloths. Marcy made the flower arrangements: some were collections of gorgeous hydrangeas, which might as well be the official flower of the Hamptons. Other vases were filled with wildflowers and various fruits. "I know, I'm so Martha," Marcy joked.

At sixish on this July evening, the guests emerged from their SUVs to find a very sexy 1955 Mercedes Gullwing 300 SL stealing the spotlight at the entrance to the party. Apparently, the car plays an integral role in the

book—but you'll have to read it to find out. Karin didn't provide any clues but did mention that she arranged for the star automobile to be at the book launch party long before she ever finished writing the book.

The stylish set then headed to the Warrens' beautiful backyard, where stilettos kept sinking into the ground and sunglasses were worn long past the point of being necessary. The newest vodka in town starred in a vodka-caviar bar, where virtually any type of martini was possible. A DJ spun groovy beach vibes as attendants served hors d'oeuvres and lots of Veuve Cliquot. Copies of the book were the party favors—everyone here needs a beach read.

"The uniqueness about entertaining in the Hamptons is that the world is your oyster," Marcy explained. "You can do so much with a big backyard and lots of good friends." (Marcy is quite famous among New York social revelers for another party she hosted in

this backyard. It was a fortieth birthday party with a circus theme that included a live elephant, a camel, ponies, jugglers, cotton candy, and other side shows.) "There is no confinement here like you find in New York City," she said.

Marcy explained that she loves entertaining because it is a chance to bring together people with interesting but different backgrounds who otherwise might not cross paths.

"People love to meet new people," she said. Marcy downplayed her role in gathering such a swanky crowd. "I just loaned my grass," she said. "Good things bring good people together. And we are all happy to promote artistic and literary endeavors."

The evening was a huge success—everyone mingled right up until their dinner reservations, no doubt discussing "who done it" and "did they do it in the car?"

TIPS FOR A BEST-SELLER BASH

Invite friends with interesting but different backgrounds whose paths might not otherwise cross.

Don't be afraid to do part of the work yourself— decorations might be a place to start.

Great music is a must— people love to come to a party that has a good vibe.

Promote good causes and celebrate others' successes.

WILD WEST SHINDIG

WHO:	"Little" Josephine and "Big" David Perry
WHAT:	The wildest of Wild West shindigs
WHEN:	From sunset until the cows come home
WHERE:	The Perrys' on the Arizona prairie
WHY:	Double birthday trouble

ANYONE WHO DRESSES UP as a gold digger is bound to host a blast of a bash. Never one to do things subtly, Josephine Perry, along with her husband, David, put the wild in Wild West with an elaborate western extravaganza at their Arizona home on the range. The far-flung festivities were orchestrated to simultaneously celebrate David's sixtieth and son Dominic's twenty-first birthdays.

Handmade western-themed save-the-date notices announced: "Yhee haw! Get all done up in yer Western duds for what we promise will be the Wildest of Wild West Shindigs." The save-the-date was necessary

months in advance because the Perrys were set on rounding up 200 friends and family who would be traveling not just across the country but also west across the Atlantic. David is the son of Fred Perry—the only Englishman ever to win Wimbledon. David's wife, "Jo," is from England as well. The pair eventually headed west, settling in Hollywood for twenty years before moving to Arizona ten years ago. "We invited people from all parts of our lives, and we incorporated that into the theme," Jo said.

When the formal invitation arrived, it coined the party a "Kick-Ass Saloon Shindig" with Wild West attire required. Jo explains that theme parties are popular among the Brits. "Having a theme party is a great idea when you have a group of people who don't know each other. Costumes create an easy conversation opener, so people will socialize more," she said.

Since the Perrys live in the Southwest, they knew the western theme would work well

because it was an easy theme for people to comply with. Everyone owns a pair of jeans, and cowboy hats are easy to come by. "Plus, people look attractive—and taller—in boots and hats," Jo added.

If costumes are indeed conversation starters, then Jo's gold-digger number, with sparkling gold shovel to match, was the talk of their custom-built town. Other guests arrived portraying a chain gang, and some of the ladies donned get-ups inspired by Madonna's rhinestone cowgirl period.

The rolling acreage at the Perrys' place lent itself to a Wild West transformation, so the entire event took place outdoors in the western town that the Perrys had constructed for the occasion. In fact, the scene resembled a Hollywood film set. Among the real cacti and desert landscape, man-made scenery included a replica of Boot Hill graveyard with RIP's dedicated to the birthday duo. At various points on the property were a saloon, a margarita cantina bar, and the Whorehouse Café. Signs directed guests to a luxury toilet—Crapper Alley—with walls covered in "Wanted" posters. Other signs pointed

to Hollywood, Southern Methodist University, where their sons attend, and London. Even the gift cart was turned into a money wagon in an effort to have every element comply with the theme. The surrounding trees were draped with fairy lights and along with the greens, reds, and yellows of the sunset shooting across the sky, gave the setting a magical feel.

Jo claims that she planned the entire weekend with German precision. The party was scheduled for 7:30 p.m. so out-of-towners could do the touristy things during the day. Dominic's university friends were escorted on a trailblazing tour through the Arizona desert, while other guests competed in a Wild West golf tournament. Also, 7:30 happened to be right before sunset, when the sky is the most beautiful backdrop.

At the entrance to the estate, guests were immediately enticed to get into the shindig spirit. A wooden archway proclaiming the premises "D & D Ranch" looked as if it had been there for years. Valets and party attendants all wore the "Dom & Dave's Kick-Ass Saloon" red T-shirts (also stating "Dolls and Brawls Nightly"

on the back). Bandanas, sheriff stars, and cowboy hats were dispersed at the door as add-ons to the guests' party outfits. And a giant replica of the party's invitation served as a guest sign-in where revelers could leave their remarks.

As the guests enjoyed scrumptious hors d'oeuvres, a quirky collection of hired characters roamed the grounds like actors on location. A John Wayne look-alike made a cameo appearance, as did a cowgirl called Pistol Packing Paula, a singing cowboy with an electric guitar riding high on a white stallion, a crooked card player performing card tricks, and a resident Indian. Hands-on attractions included a mechanical bull and a high-striker game with rankings beginning at "sissy" level.

Jo claims that she planned the entire weekend with German precision.

Hands-on attractions included a mechanical bull and a high-striker game with rankings beginning at "sissy" level.

TIPS FROM THE WILD WEST

Create a fun setting that will engender conversation. Lighting and sound are important elements.

Costumes and conversations go hand in hand and promote mixing among all age groups.

Make the meal an integral part of the event. A leisurely pace is most enjoyable.

For large parties at your home, hiring security is a wise precautionary measure.

Please join us at our home for
Dom and Dave's
Kick-Ass Saloon Shindig

Saturday, May 17th
7:30 p.m.

Wild West attire required!

RSVP by April 1st

When it was time for the main event—dinner—a semicircle of wagons created the venue. Although the meal was come-and-get-it buffet style, Jo chose to have assigned seating. Table names were displayed attached to horseshoes and included titles appropriate to the group of guests seated at the table. For example: Dallas Cowboys, Beverly Hillbillies, In-laws and Outlaws. The place cards referred to each person as "Big Al" or "Little Sarah," etc., depending on gender. Young people were seated right along with older folk. Jo points out that the younger crowd tends not to drink as much that way, even if they have just turned twenty-one.

The food itself included ribs, chicken, and everything else you would expect at a cowboy feast, including baked beans served in petite silver pails. Toasts were made during the main course, and then a jazz/western trio provided the entertainment on a stage and dance floor that resembled a rodeo rink. Dessert included fruits and cowboy cookies in the shape of hats and boots. There were also an ice cream parlor and an espresso and coffee cafe.

Finally, the night turned into a disco. Guests gave the party rave reviews and didn't mosey home until 2:30 a.m. But before they left, each guest's key chain was attached with a bolo tie. Most returned to the Perrys' the next morning for brunch and an open house.

Jo theorizes that well-thought-out parties show the guests how important they are and end up being the most fun. "Success in the details, that is what makes a party special," she said. In the end, it was Jo's creative attention to detail that enabled the Perrys to strike gold with this event.

FASHION FANTASY AT THE BECK HOUSE

WHO: Brian Bolke and his fashion house, Forty Five Ten

WHAT: A Narcisco Rodriguez fantasy fete

WHEN: A Sunday evening wake-up call

WHERE: Philip Johnson's glowing Beck House

WHY: To benefit the Child and Family Guidance Center

"ALWAYS THROW THE TYPE OF PARTY that you'd like to go to," advises Brian Bolke, co-owner of Dallas fashion mecca Forty Five Ten and one of the city's most sought-after event masters. And from the likes of the parties that Brian hosts, it appears that the type of party he likes to go to is the kind the rest of us dream of getting invited to. Another morsel of his party-planning advice: "Give people what they can't get at just any event."

Brian has a way of brilliantly succeeding in both of these mantras. For him it was business as usual as he stunned the city with his unusual charity benefit for the

> "It is such an architecturally sophisticated house that what you didn't do was more important than what you did."

Child and Family Guidance Center. The event starred fashion minimalist master Narcisco Rodriguez at the Philip Johnson–designed Beck House on what would have otherwise been a sleepy Sunday night.

The mystical evening unfolded like this: Brian, who is extremely involved in this charity, decided to orchestrate a benefit that would involve his chic store and Narcisco Rodriguez, who was being honored in Dallas for his selection as Womenswear Designer of the Year. Since this was the first time Forty Five Ten had hosted a charity event, Brian planned the evening from scratch. Forty Five Ten provided a full-on runway show with Narcisco's modern, architecturally precise, simple-looking yet complex designs as the focal point.

Brian infused the occasion with a huge element of surprise: the venue was the Beck House, itself a work of modern art with the signature cubed shape and arches for which Philip Johnson's architecture is famous. Virtually no one had seen this home in twenty years, but it changed ownership and was suddenly available for the cause before the new owners embarked on a three-year restoration.

Brian enlisted New York event designers Antony Todd and Todd Fiscus to aid in the magical metamorphosis.

"It is such an architecturally sophisticated house that what you didn't do was more important than what you did," Brian explained. They went with a stark white modern décor, which made perfect sense for the design of the house and also of the clothing collection. Since the house was empty, they brought in white cube-shaped ottomans for seating. One entire wall is actually a waterfall, so water was incorporated into the decoration as well. White votives floated in all sorts of clear bottles and on glass serving structures. All the flowers (provided by Avant Garden) were white, with gardenias floating near the staircase and strung as chandeliers, and thousands of orchids springing up from assorted asymmetrical clear vases. Brian points out

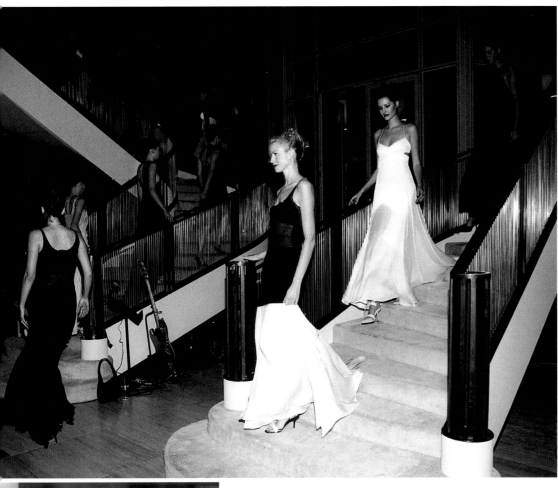

The chic shop Forty Five Ten provided a full-on runway show with Narciso's architecturally precise yet simple-looking fashions as the focal point.

tension is one of his favorite words and is how he describes the dynamics of the evening. With this untested venue, he explained that he didn't know if the single bathroom downstairs would suffice, whether the acoustics would accommodate the crowd and the entertainment, or if a model would fall down the dramatic double staircase during the runway show. No one even checked to see if the gas was on in the house until 5 p.m. the night of the party. (It wasn't, and emergency backup plans were rolled into action.)

Guests were equally in the dark. Since this was a first-time event, no one knew who would be there, what would be worn, or even what the evening was about. By the time the three hundred unsuspecting guests arrived, including charity chairman and television's advice guru

another parallel: one of Narciso's best-known dresses, made famous by actress Jennifer Connelly, was a black gown with a single white gardenia.

"By nature, anything safe is not fun," Brian says. "The best things in life are on the edge of disaster." In that sense,

whether to break the energy for the fashion show. Afterwards, each room in the house contained a different segment of the dinner buffet, which was created by a local restaurant, Abacus. There was cheese in the dining room, sushi in the study, sweets . . . well, you get the idea. Then guests were captivated by New York–based singing sensation Sasha Lazard, who does a sultry pop-opera sound mixed with tribal rhythms.

After several exhilarating hours and a couple of encores, delighted guests took home souvenir Narcisco-designed bags, which also included a T-shirt by the designer and Sasha's latest CD.

There are so many society events in Dallas that only a few stand out in people's memories, and this was one of those rare productions that succeeded in raising eyebrows, dropping jaws, and creating a citywide buzz.

Dr. Phil McGraw and family, the scene at the house was surreal. The party started with hors d'oeuvres accompanied by several different cocktails, including mini bottles of champagne with straws. By all accounts, the mood was so intoxicating that the hosts momentarily debated

TIPS FOR BECOMING THE "HOST OF THE TOWN"

Always *throw* the type of party that you'd like to attend.

Create spontaneous and edgy parties for maximum energy—if you stick with what's safe, you're missing out on a lot of fun.

Depending on the venue, sometimes what you don't do for décor is just as important as what you do.

Dare to be different—give people what they won't get at other events.

SUMMER SHOWERS

WHO: Interior decorator Jan Showers and husband Jim Showers

WHAT: A stylish summer dinner

WHEN: An elegant evening in early summer

WHERE: The Showers' ultra-glamorous townhouse in Dallas

WHY: Every day is an occasion to celebrate

IN BOTH DECORATING AND ENTERTAINING, Jan Showers has an ongoing love affair with glamour. Look closely and you'll see that certain themes resonate in her creations, whether she is designing a dinner party or a living room. You'll see more than recurring objects of desire—colorful Venetian glass, '40s French antiques, tussled flower arrangements; you'll also discover parallel philosophies. In Jan's view, things should be beautiful yet understated, never flashy. She believes it is personal style, rather than

Hints of old Hollywood allure carry over from Jan's taste in décor to her artful entertaining style.

money spent, that makes a room, a party, or even an outfit glamorous.

Hints of old Hollywood allure carry over from Jan's taste in décor to her artful entertaining style, and she explains that her personal style is in part inspired by the elegance of the era when Katharine Hepburn graced the big screen. She also finds inspiration in family tradition. "I am very influenced by my mother, who was the consummate entertainer," Jan says. "She knew how to make everything look and taste absolutely perfect. Every time I give a party or even cook a small, intimate dinner, I am inspired by her." During one of Jan's cozy summer dinner parties, she shared a few of her favorite things and her take on entertaining with style.

"Make sure invitations look original and are enticing enough so everyone will want to be at your party," Jan advises. When her travels take her to Manhattan, she stocks up

To request the pleasure of your company

for *Cocktails and Dinner*

on *June 4 at 8 o'clock*

at *Christopher Place*

Jan and Jim

on Mrs. John L. Strong invitations, which can be found at Barney's or at the designer's personal store. The selections include '40s-style caricatures, all terrifically glam. Tonight's invitation depicts a clever purple butler serving martinis. Professional printing is not required; Jan likes writing them by hand or using a calligrapher.

For setting an elegant table, Jan is perhaps best known for her passion for Venetian glass. "Venetian glass centerpieces add sparkle to any room, and when accompanied by votives, the reflections are dazzling," she explains. Usually a few subtle flowers accompany the glass, but the glass makes a dramatic statement on its own.

On the dining table and across the house, Jan makes sure that flower arrangements look anything but arranged. Although florist Ron Shultz has been her secret weapon for years, she explains, "Highly contrived arrangements are not my thing. I like them to look as though they just came out of my garden and as if I could have done them myself." The effect of these elements—the glass and the flowers—adds color and richness to the setting.

Contrast among tables is another of Jan's favorite techniques. "If you have more than one table, use different china, flatware, linens and table decorations on each," she advises. "The color schemes for each table should vary and use different flowers."

For the menu, Jan recommends meeting with a caterer in plenty of time. Personally, she won't commit to a party date without checking the availability of her favorite cater-er, The Food Company. With their help she selects at least three or four hors d'oeuvres to be passed during cocktails. "Make sure the hors d'oeuvres are tiny," she says. "Ladies don't like to have to take but one bite." Guests should always be offered a drink upon arrival, and she advises having a complete bar. "The cocktail hour should be no longer than 45 minutes—no one wants to stand too long or eat and drink too much before dinner," she says.

True to her signature style, Jan likes the main courses to look unpretentious, as if she

picked it up at the market and cooked it her-self. She advocates the importance of season-al cooking, always with top-of-the-line ingre-dients. Some cold-weather favorites include fish potpie and old-fashioned fried chicken.

"The color schemes for each table should
vary and use different flowers."

"Champagne should always be offered with dessert . . ."

JAN'S TIPS FOR A GLAMOROUS GET-TOGETHER

Use unique and original invitations that will make guests want to attend your event.

Venetian glass centerpieces add glamour to any table.

From flowers to food, all the elements of entertaining should be high quality but not pretentious.

End the evening with bubbles—champagne is a festive treat for every occasion.

In warm months she likes to serve lighter meals, beginning with a cold first course. In that way, the first course can be on the table before guests are seated. Overall, she explains, "I love the juxtaposition of a really elegant table setting with a simple but very tasty menu."

Adding even more sparkle to her table, all dinners at the Showers' home end with a little sparkling wine. "Champagne should always be offered with dessert—your guests will think the evening even more festive and the dessert will taste even more wonderful." Besides, is there anything more glamorous than a flute full of bubbles?

CELEBRATING A YOUNG TALENT

WHO: Neiman Marcus and *PaperCity* magazine

WHAT: A far-out fete featuring fashion designer Zac Posen

WHEN: On the eve of Posen's debut trunk show at Neiman Marcus

WHERE: The Mansion on Turtle Creek

WHY: To welcome a young talent to the fashion world

LEAVE IT TO NEIMAN MARCUS vice president of public relations Ken Downing to invent a theme that takes a whole sentence to state and several paragraphs to explain. "This is about an eccentric rock star with a country mansion outside of London who invites friends over to celebrate the arrival of his groovy fashion friend who has come to visit," Ken explained. From that fantasy came not a fashion photo shoot, but one far-out party.

The usual décor of the mansion on Turtle Creek was turned upside down to accommodate this upscale celebration.

In this scenario, the groovy fashion friend is none other than designer Zac Posen, fashion's man-of-the-moment. His first runway show was described as having "a front row with more star power than a Lakers game." And the mansion outside of London? It's actually Dallas's premier hotel, The Mansion on Turtle Creek. With its aristocratic and oh-so-exclusive ambiance, the hotel on a normal night is the last place you would look to find hip rocker types. So Neiman Marcus and *PaperCity* magazine, who doubled up to throw this wacky welcome for Posen, turned The Mansion upside down.

"Throwing a party is like theater: you have to set the stage. The guests are actors in the play," Downing philosophizes. The hosts wanted the party theme to be much like the attitude of Posen's creations: very modern but with homage to history, mixed with just the right amount of whimsy. As Posen himself has described his timeless designs, "You can't tell if they're from the past, the present, or the future."

Setting the slightly mad tone for the evening, the invitation was filled with quirky quotes from English literature and pictured

Guests were invited for hors d'oeuvres and cocktails
(in cocktail attire), and the invitation clearly designated
pink as the color of the evening.

fictional country-mansion servants dusting and serving martinis. "A well-designed invitation doesn't have to say much," Ken says. "It sets the mood—witty vs. serious, formal vs. casual." Ken believes the invitation should also preview the menu and the color of the event.

Guests were invited for hors d'oeuvres and cocktails (in cocktail attire), and the invitation clearly designated pink as the color of the evening. "Everyone looks good in pink," said Ken.

For The Mansion's elaborate makeover, the hotel's usual décor was replaced with racy animal-skin rugs and throws, pink Asian parasols, and funky furniture from all corners of the globe—packed in to make the famed hotel look like a futuristic home. David Quadrini of Angstrom Gallery switched out twenty of the classic oil paintings that usually adorn The Mansion bar for pieces of modern art from his gallery. Blasé lighting was swapped in favor of red and purple bulbs. Not much resembled the old once the transformation of the manse was complete, but one important

Asian furnishings, along with animal-skin throws and rugs, created a funky, exotic ambiance.

factor helped achieve the desired result: they started with a mansion to begin with. "Don't re-create Versailles inside a gymnasium," Ken proclaims with regard to venue. "Look for a location with what you want and then embellish it. Don't build a box within a box." He also points out, "When you see the magic, there is no magic." Meaning, don't forget to cover up extension cords, cables, and the like.

Adding to the over-the-top antics of this party, a slew of staff was hired to "act" in the production. The 700 partygoers arrived to see gardeners and window washers tending to the outside of this supposed country mansion. Inside, a fleet of butlers in black and white and maids dressed in pink hammed it up while dancing and feather dusting around the guests. British accents were in the air as waiters wearing pink ties served pink cosmopolitans and what seemed

PARTY TIPS FROM NEIMAN'S KEN DOWNING

The invitation should reflect the party's color and preview the menu.

Choose the venue that is best suited to your theme—don't build a box within a box.

Consider inviting a gallery to provide fresh art for the evening.

Guests should see the magic—not what went in to creating it. Keep cords, cables, and other building blocks behind the scenes.

like rivers of champagne. Models wearing Posen's eccentric yet elegant creations posed as chic houseguests.

Just as you'd envision at a fantasy mansion party, the feast featured a roasted pig with essential apple in its chops, along with empanadas, English sandwiches, and smoked turkey biscuits with cranberry sauce. Chef Dean Fearing was happy to oblige the theme with his festive pink chef's coat custom-ordered for the occasion.

As guests danced the night away to the sounds of a band called Mr. Pink, Posen himself made an effort to personally greet every attendee. As he told local media, "It's very inspiring to meet the people who wear the clothing. And I am in the service business, so I have to be responsive and hopefully fulfill their fantasies."

Zac fans must have been inspired by all that carrying on at The Mansion—the next day they showed up at downtown Neiman's with cards ready for the show. By day's end, more than $100,000 worth of orders had been placed, including the sale of one $15,000 dress. Now, that's an after party.

FASHION AMBASSADORS

WHO: Neiman Marcus's Ken Downing and Sam Saladino

WHAT: Intimate dinners at home

WHEN: It's an ongoing affair

WHERE: Home sweet home in Dallas

WHY: Entertaining members of fashion's inner circles

TUCKED AWAY JUST OUTSIDE of downtown Dallas in a charming, almost tree house–like 1950s residence in Kessler Park, Neiman Marcus public relations czar Ken Downing and sales associate Sam Saladino hold court. As Dallas's unofficial ambassadors to fashion's international A-list, the duo find themselves frequently entertaining designers, artists, and other creative types who are passing through town.

"It's more fun to entertain out-of-town guests at home than to take them out to dinner," Ken says. "People tend to let their hair down here." He believes

Injecting intellectualism into the table décor,
pieces are often used for purposes other than the obvious.

that home entertaining also allows guests to get a feel for how the host lives.

Formally trained in fashion design, Ken is the visualist of the two. While growing up in Seattle, he first developed an eye for designing the table by observing his mother's stylish luncheons at their home. Later he spent years perfecting his craft in Neiman's visual design department. He describes the décor of his own house as "a modern mix with overdone moments," and the look is the same whether guests are present or not: he doesn't believe in artificially dressing it up for entertaining.

Sam's fine-tuned culinary talents—gained mostly through working at his family's Italian restaurant—complement Ken's visual expertise to create a cohesive collaboration for entertaining and dining.

The table at Ken and Sam's place looks nothing like a typical store-bought place setting. Instead, their glamorous Christian Dior and Ralph Lauren pieces are elegantly integrated with antiques and family heirlooms. "We've been collecting vintage Morano glass for twelve years, and our silver is Ken's family's," Sam

explains. "We like to mix the old with the new."

They also like to mix unusual shapes and make them work together. Ken favors interesting decanters and never leaves beverages or accoutrements in their original containers. Unique serving pieces are another of his collecting passions, and cocktails are always presented on individual trays.

Injecting intellectualism into the table décor, pieces are often used for purposes other than the obvious. For instance, atop the cherub cake plates passed down from Ken's mother, guests are more likely to find cheese, fruit, and chocolate truffles than cakes or pies. Decorative bowls are filled with quirky conversation starters; for example, a colorful glass egg might be intermingled with real eggs. Ken prefers this sort of centerpiece to floral arrangements. While a handful of flowers usually beautifies the table, bouquets play a much larger role in other rooms of the house.

Creative party favors are often tied into the place settings. "I always have little tidbits waiting for each guest," Ken says. He suggests using something monogrammed or personal so it can double as a place card. Candles, notepads, and frames are a few favorites.

Both Ken and Sam believe in being very hands-on. They don't hire help unless they are hosting a large group, which is not often because they are partial to small dinner parties. "Entertaining at home needs to be a charming affair, and having too many servers takes the personal touch out of it," Ken says. And no caterers are necessary—everything they serve is homemade by Sam, except for the exquisite Neiman Marcus chocolates they bring home from the store.

The menu is always designed around a great entrée, usually something traditional like beef and potatoes or macaroni and cheese but with a modern twist. Among their modern art and sleek furniture, they retained certain features original to the home, such as the oven, which Sam uses exclusively.

"For inspiration, we try to envision the cocktail parties that took place here in the '50s and '60s, with martinis and pigs-in-a-blanket," Sam says. After the entrée, Ken revamps the table for the cheese and chocolate course. Most

evenings end with coffee served in the living room in front of their grand fireplace, with Tigerlily the cat, and dogs Nicky and BuBulasha sharing in the fun.

And in the spirit of bygone days, the house does not have a single television. Although you'd never guess it by their larger-than-life personalities and fashion-forward ways, Ken and Sam's philosophy when it comes to entertaining at home is to keep things intimate and casual, simple and sensible. One might term their style "vintage entertaining" but with updated wardrobes.

TIPS FOR FASHIONABLE DINING AT HOME

It isn't necessary to artificially dress up one's home for entertaining.

In decorating and in entertaining, mix the simplicity of yesteryear with the elegance and style of today.

Too many helpers detract from the intimacy.

Personalized party favors can serve as coveted place cards.

BARNSTABLE BROWN KENTUCKY DERBY

WHO: Tricia Barnstable Brown and twin sister Cyb

WHAT: A star-studded southern gala

WHEN: Kentucky Derby eve

WHERE: At home in the Deep South

WHY: Raising funds for diabetes research

THE KENTUCKY DERBY TRADITIONALLY draws a conservative crowd, elegantly decked out in glamorous hats and preppy horsy attire. It's not the type of scene that one would expect to attract the likes of Anna Nicole Smith or Pamela Anderson. But thanks in part to Tricia Barnstable Brown, whose yearly fund-raiser for diabetes research has long been considered *the* party of horseracing's most important weekend, Hollywood has invaded the Kentucky Derby.

Tricia and her twin sister, Priscilla, aka Cyb, were first introduced to national stardom at age twenty when Tricia

was competing in the Miss USA Pageant with Cyb in the audience cheering her on. When Tricia was named second runner-up, the camera panned to Cyb, and in one of those only-in-Hollywood twists of fate, Bob Hope happened to see them on television. They soon became part of Hope's Christmas show that visited American soldiers serving in Vietnam. The next year the two were cast as the original Doublemint Twins in a national television campaign for chewing gum that aired over seven years. Decades later, the twins' southern hospitality has turned the Barnstable Brown Derby Eve Gala into a yearly pilgrimage for countless celebrities.

It all started as a 500-person gathering at Tricia's home in 1989 to benefit a cause that later became extremely personal when her husband was diagnosed with diabetes. Over the years the party grew, as did the money raised for research; but despite the current 900-plus guest list, Tricia continues to hold the event at her home each year. "I just keep adding tent after tent after tent in my backyard," she told local media. "The

Kentucky Derby has a lot of different aspects, one of which is a stately elegance that is rooted in tradition. The ambiance of the party revolves around 'southern hospitality,' and I think having the party in my home portrays that."

Each year the party takes on a new theme, 2003 being the year of dance. On arrival, guests were treated to performances by children's dance troups taking place on several stages constructed across the lawn. Inside the party, seating for different donor levels was distinguished by dance categories, and each section's décor matched its type of dance: the salsa section was done up in sassy red; disco-level

TIPS FOR A FUND-RAISER WORTHY OF THE WINNER'S CIRCLE

Choose a date when some additional big event might serve as an incentive for your out-of-town guests to make the trip.

Play up your location's regional personality with flair.

Use your connections to achieve maximum attendance—the bigger the stars, the brighter the party, the more donations to the cause.

Involve the local community in entertainment, décor, menu and corporate sponsorships.

donors dined at tables covered with psychedelic fabrics set up under sparkling disco balls; centerpieces in the tap section were wine chillers in the shape of top hats.

Despite all the work the hostesses put into the decorations, the real eye candy is always the guests. This evening's star-studded group included members of NSYNC, Anna Nicole Smith, George Strait, Janet Jackson, La Toya Jackson, Stone Phillips, Pamela Anderson, Larry King, Tammy Faye Messner (formerly Baker), Slash of Guns n' Roses fame, Troy Aikman, Bo Derek, and many more. And they don't stand around sipping mint juleps, either. Highlights of the event are the celebrity performances, which (along with the media frenzy) makes the gala seem more like the MTV Music Awards than a Derby party. This year the evening's most memorable moment was the performance by Kid Rock, Travis Tritt, and Taylor Dayne onstage together singing "Sweet Home Alabama."

One reminder that the party really is in Kentucky, after all, is the southern comfort food served at lavish buffet stations. Selections included cornucopia salad, beef tenderloin with Henry Bain sauce, chicken Duxelle, grilled shrimp and bow tie pasta, Kentucky corn pudding, creamed spinach, and hot rolls. Sixteen different desserts and a cappuccino bar provided sweet endings.

Apparently the gala has all the right elements to please even the most sought-after stars. Joey Fatone of NSYNC explains, "This charity event is put together so well that everyone feels the excitement and warmth in the air. It feels like an awards show when you pull up to the house with thousands of people in the street all waiting to see celebrities. Then just walking up to the house is an experience, with kids from all over the community doing songs from Broadway musicals—this sets the tone for the entire party. Inside everyone goes up and sings onstage and just enjoys each other's company. I love southern hospitality—this is one party I plan on attending every year." Horse races? What horse races?

SENTIMENTAL JOURNEYS

WHO: Longue Vue House and Gardens

WHAT: Sentimental Journeys, a benefit with international elegance and allure

WHEN: Every eighteen months

WHERE: New Orleans, Louisiana—where the journey begins

WHY: To inspire the pursuit of beauty and civic responsibility

MARK TWAIN ONCE EXPLAINED, "Twenty years from now you will be more disappointed by the things that you didn't do than the ones that you did do, so throw off the bowlines. Sail away from the safe harbor. Catch the trade winds in your sails. Explore. Discover. Dream." No other charity event captures this attitude quite like Sentimental Journeys, the major fund-raising event for Longue Vue House and Gardens, a historic estate in New Orleans created by

philanthropists Mr. and Mrs. Edgar Stern from 1939 to 1942.

Longue Vue, the Sterns' former residence, is now a museum and a nonprofit, educational and cultural institution where children and adults participate in hands-on activities to learn about gardening, conservation, and ecology. Its mission is "to use the historic and artistic legacy of Longue Vue and its creators to educate and inspire people to pursue beauty and civic responsibility in their lives." In order to create the most appropriate benefit for the charity, the organizers took a page from the Sterns' fascinating legacy to come up with the Sentimental Journeys theme. "The Sterns were explorers who were very inspired by cultural activities," says Bonnie Goldblum, executive director of Longue Vue. "Sentimental Journeys started with the intent to support Longue Vue's programs while highlighting the Sterns' love of adventure, education, and culture."

Everything about this weekend-long event relates to the romantic, real-life

journey that the Sterns took around the world in 1936–37 to celebrate fifteen years of marriage. The gala derives its name from the title of a memoir privately published by the Sterns to document their travels—"A Sentimental Journey Through France and Italy and Other Countries." One of the trademarks of the benefit, which is pictured on the invitation, is a gold cigarette case given to Mrs. Stern by her husband in memory of their once-in-a-lifetime trip. The case is engraved with a map of the world and adorned with ruby chips indicating each of their stops on the adventure. It is inscribed, "To E.R.S. with Everlasting Gratitude for the Unforgettable Experience of a Sentimental Journey from E.B.S." Although the main focus of the gala weekend is the auctioning of thirty exotic trips designed to delight modern-day

adventurers, the arrival of so many sup-
porters from around the globe is really
what makes the event a grand experience.
Guests have the good fortune to experience world-class cuisine and culture of
near and far, even if they aren't fortunate
enough to make the winning bid for one
of the journeys.

This year's festivities began with a
patron party in the gardens of a private
home in downtown New Orleans. Making
the outdoor atmosphere even more magical were the elaborate floral decorations
designed by internationally renowned
florist Marcel Wolterinck of Holland.
Several stations were set up in the garden
where guests could sample a blending of
German, French, and Louisiana culinary
traditions provided by chef John Besh of New
Orleans' Restaurant August. Artisanal cheeses
were presented by Max McCalman, who serves
as maître fromager of Picholine and Artisanal
Restaurants in New York, and who is one of
the world's leading authorities on cheese.
Several vineyards were also represented, and
guests experienced tastings of many exquisite
private reserves and vintage wines.
International blues legend Mose Allison's
unforgettable performance under the stars

Not only is the entertainment international in flavor, but so is the food. The guests also come from around the globe to this week-long fund-raising event.

The energy of the evening,
as one might expect,
peaked with the live auction.

made the evening a treat to yet another of the senses.

Saturday evening brought the seated dinner and the highly anticipated auction, which began with cocktails inside another of New Orleans' prominent private homes. There the guests were treated to a performance by Cambodian dancers and musicians showcasing the traditions and culture of their native homeland. The guests then moved outside to the tented main event, which was dramatically decorated with stark white furniture, linens, vases, and candelabras, contrasted by clear glassware. Marcel Wolterinck created innovative palm trees and balanced elaborate white floral arrangements atop glass vases that, at several feet high, towered over the guests. The dance floor was hand-painted with a swirling white design to match the distinctive décor.

French chef Eric Branger of the New Orleans Ritz Carlton and Ron Siegel of Masa Restaurant in San Francisco combined forces to prepare the evening's multicourse dinner, which was accompanied by selections from several California wineries. Afterwards guests grooved to the Latin, classical, and jazz sounds of Pink Martini, an Oregon-based band whose popularity has led to recent appearances on such television shows as *The Sopranos* and *The West Wing*.

The energy of the evening, as one might

expect, peaked with the live auction. Guests bid enthusiastically on photo safaris in Kenya, whitewater rafting in Chile, stays at French châteaux, travel across the Caribbean by a private 138-foot yacht, entrance to the Fall Fashion Shows in New York, and many other adventures that follow in the Sterns' footsteps. "The trips really do present once-in-a-lifetime opportunities," Ms. Goldblum explains. "Through this travel, relationships are born and continue to grow." In addition to raising money for Longue Vue, she explains that by creating such bonds, the event has had a broader impact nationally and internationally than they ever anticipated at Sentimental Journey's inception. And that's not to overlook the beneficial impact it has right at home on

TIPS TO BETTER YOUR BENEFIT

Educate your guests while you entertain them—bring in experts to enhance the experience.

Adding international elements makes any event more exotic.

A live auction is entertainment in itself, as well as a profitable technique to raise funds.

Make sure guests understand the history and purposes of the charity. A sentimental story may help distinguish it from other worthy causes.

the recipients of Longue Vue's programs—because whether in a far away land or your own backyard, one can always explore, discover, and dream.

THE POWER OF PEPPERMINT

WHO: Yours truly, Kimberly Schlegel

WHAT: Brunch for busy friends

WHEN: A few calm moments in the middle of holiday madness

WHERE: High-rise in Dallas

WHY: To celebrate the season and all of life's little gifts

BETWEEN DASHING THROUGH THE MALL, churning out holiday cards, and getting dolled-up for those endless seasonal soirees, sometimes we forget to slow down and reflect on the true meaning of the holidays. The "Peppermint Party" was a way for me to gather close friends and treat them to a breather from the December madness, while also focusing on one of life's most precious gifts—friendship—something that we should celebrate during the holidays and all year long.

Your friends will appreciate your
efforts to host something special
for them, despite small quarters.

Twelve friends received a red-and-white-striped card with white overlay printed in green and tied together with a matching polka-dot ribbon. The lighthearted invitation announced brunch at my high-rise apartment to celebrate the spirit of the season.

Entertaining in apartments can be a bit intimidating because you generally don't have a lot of space to work with. But that doesn't mean you should avoid it altogether. Your friends will appreciate your efforts to host something special for them, despite small

quarters. I don't have a large dining room table in my apartment, so I brought in two rectangular tables and put them together to accommodate twelve. One long, white linen tablecloth covering both gave the appearance of a single, elegant dining table. Red chairs with white seat cushions completed the setting. It all worked perfectly for the intimate seated brunch.

Huge hurricane vases filled with peppermints made cheerful and inexpensive centerpieces. Red-and-white unscented candles were placed between them for added detail. Red napkins at each place setting were tied with white pom-poms, and the result was a fittingly festive table without the use of traditional holiday decorations. Also diverging from the usual was a flower arrangement made up of dozens of carnations in the shape of a holiday tree. And Lola, my dog, was a decoration herself in her miniature Santa suit with fur trim. "Refreshing and original without being overdone," is how guest Christy Smith described the decorations. "It's nice to see that a fantastic party can be

> "It's nice to see that a fantastic party can be achieved without spending a fortune."

achieved without spending a fortune."

As brunch progressed, each course was served with appropriate glassware and plates in red, clear, or a swirled combination of the two hues. Even the food and spirits flirted with the peppermint theme: one course was a white truffle soup with tomato accent created in a striped pattern; the winter greens salad was served with cranberry vinaigrette; and dessert was divine peppermint ice cream accompanied by strawberries. Raspberries floated in the champagne, and hot chocolate was, of course, served with peppermint Schnapps.

My favorite aspect of the celebration was not the décor or the food, but the personal moments that we shared. On the back of each place card I had printed a

Although the decorations were budget-conscious, every detail was attended to with style.

TIPS FOR HOSTING A WARM HOLIDAY PARTY

Provoke meaningful conversation by printing individual topics or questions for the guests on their place cards.

Unscented candles should be used on dining tables so as not to interfere with the scents of the cuisine or irritate sensitive noses.

Create unusual yet festive centerpieces by using the traditional colors of the season together with not-so-traditional objects.

Give guests the gift of relaxation and reflection.

Two tables can be disguised as one larger table with a single tablecloth covering both.

different conversation starter, such as, "Share your most treasured holiday memory" or "Tell of your favorite holiday tradition." One by one, each guest contributed a story based on her assigned topic. This kept the real importance of the holidays in everyone's thoughts, and also enabled the guests to get to know each other on a more intimate level. Allison Hopkins commented, "It was a great way to enjoy and share traditions of our families with

a group of close friends." Another friend, actress Janine Turner, playfully described the party as the "the power of peppermint" and noted that the gathering of friends "touched her soul."

A peppermint-scented candle was given to each guest as a party favor to remind her of the sentimental gathering as she returned to the hustle and bustle of the season. I attached a red-and-white polka-dot ribbon on each with a personalized sticker that said, simply, "With love, Kim." The love of good friends, after all, is one ingredient of the holidays that we should always make time for.

IT'S A SMALL WORLD AFTER ALL

WHO: Margaret Hedburg, ball director, and debutante Kari Schlegel

WHAT: The International Debutante Ball

WHEN: December 2002

WHERE: The Waldorf-Astoria Grand Ballroom, New York City

WHY: Making a bow to society

IT ALL STARTED WITH A COMMENT made by Consuela Vanderbilt, who later married the ninth Duke of Marlborough. While reminiscing about the two-week trip she endured long before air travel in order to make her debut in England, she noted, "Girls don't realize what a wonderful opportunity they have today to fly around the globe to attend each other's parties." Beatrice Dinsmore Joyce, a New York socialite and humanitarian who had a penchant for pageantry and

grand parties, heard this observation and was instantly inspired to create the International Debutante Ball. The ball made its own debut in 1954 and, as they say, the rest is history. And what a glorious and rich history it is!

Director of the ball, Margaret Hedberg, who also happens to be founder Beatrice Dinsmore Joyce's niece, explains that debutante balls in general have evolved since the '50s and '60s when the balls were private affairs. "Now almost every ball is a charitable event." She explains, "So while the traditions are still there, the girls come mainly to raise money for charity, to have fun, and to spend time with family. They are more interested in meeting other girls from around the world—to meet friends rather than husbands."

Since its inception, over two thousand young women representing seventy-two countries and forty-four

The impossibly deep Texas dip is executed with grace by debutante Kari Schlegel.

The International Debutante Ball
has long been hailed a highlight
of New York's winter social season.

states have been formally introduced to society at this social and patriotic event. Each debutante is accompanied by two escorts: one of her choosing and one assigned member from the United States Air Force, Coast Guard, Military or Naval Academies, who carries the flag of the country or state the debutante represents. The Soldiers', Sailors', Marines', and Airmen's Club of New York City is the main beneficiary of the ball, another aspect that adds to the national and international importance of the event.

The International Debutante Ball has long been hailed a highlight of New York's winter social season. More than one thousand guests attend the formal affair, which takes place every other year at the Waldorf-Astoria. Like the notion of the debutante ball itself, the elements of this gala are deeply rooted in tradition. The décor and the

The winter wonderland
setting truly captured
the magic that is Manhattan
in December.

entertainment have remained unchanged since the event's inaugural beginnings.

The dramatic multilevel ballroom is elaborately decorated in shades of pink, representing femininity, and silver, symbolizing elegance—a color scheme that was introduced by the event's founder. "We want the young people to feel like this is truly a glamorous event," Mrs. Hedberg said. "We strive to create a fantasyland feel with the flowers and the décor. However, since the goal is to raise money for charity, we have to make sure that we don't spend a fortune creating the setting." This year, splendid pink linens, clear glassware, and tall floral arrangements of pink roses and white orchids with silver accents created the stunning tabletops. And the debutantes carried similar bouquets of pink roses with painted silver leaves. Garlands of lights were draped across the balcony loges of the ballroom. The stage was decorated with frosted white Christmas trees and lighted snowflakes dangled overhead. The winter wonderland setting truly captured the magic that is Manhattan in December.

Anyone who has ever danced the night

While high-society traditions are firmly in place at the ball, there is no lack of fun. The dancing is done to the big-band sounds of Lester Lanin and his orchestra.

Mrs. Hedberg explained. "The ball is about the debutantes." This requires soft music during dinner, then as the ceremony takes place, the band orchestrates personalized music selected to reflect each debutante's homeland as she is presented. Finally, after the presentation ceremony, the musical sets are traditionally so upbeat and alluring that dancing the night away at this ball is a common occurrence.

This year sixty-three girls debuted at the event. International debutantes hailing from Austria, France, England, Greece, Iceland, Italy, and Scotland took part in the ball, including several members of royalty. My sister, Kari Schlegel, who debuted this year, said

away at the International Deb Ball has experienced the big band sounds of Lester Lanin and his orchestra, who have provided the music for the ball since the beginning. "While some orchestras are about the conductor putting on a show, this orchestra is experienced in making sure that the music's focus is the event itself,"

that the best part of her experience was meeting so many people from all over the world. "The girls being presented, their families, and their guests made for such an interesting and diverse group," she said. "It was a fascinating mix of cultures in a beautiful setting." Adding a bit of Texas culture to the mix, the debutantes from

Dallas and Houston, as they were presented, performed the traditional "Texas Dip," which is an almost impossibly low curtsy. Each time a girl from Texas was presented, there was excitement in the air as the guests awaited the unique bow.

It is up to each girl to make the ball experience uniquely her own—from picking a white gown that suits her style to entertaining her guests. Kari made her dress selection a family affair, bringing several of us along to help choose from among the collections at Neiman Marcus' wedding salon. For weeks prior to the event, she prepared gift packages for the twenty-one family members and friends who would travel to New York to attend the ball. "I wanted to find gifts that reflected New York and that also made useful souvenirs," she explained. The thoughtful selection included pocket-sized maps of New York City, Manhattan-skyline snow globes, cookies in the shape of Bloomingdale's shoppers, Zagat's restaurant and nightlife guides, Empire State Building notepads, taxicab keychains, elegant black-and-white photographs of the snow-covered city, disposable cameras, and jewel-encrusted frames engraved with the

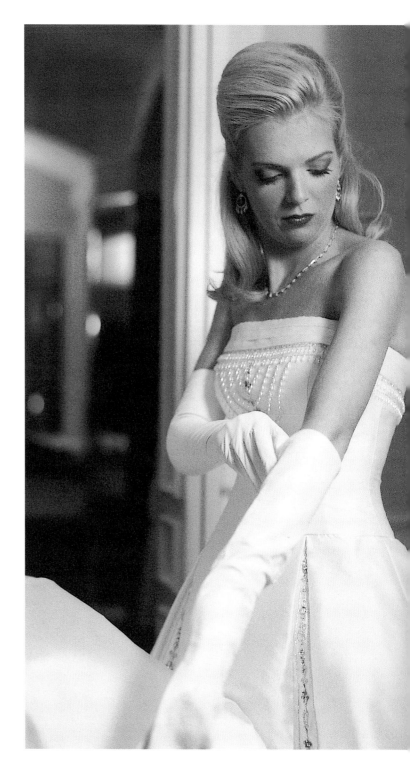

event's date. Also waiting for each of the guests upon arrival were personal notes from Kari, thanking each for their support and attendance at the historic ball.

A debut marks a milestone in the lives of many young women, and the enchanting setting and historic significance of this ball makes the experience all the more memorable. The International Debutante Ball brings the year to an elegant ending while signifying new beginnings and instigating new friendships.

TIPS FOR A FORMAL CHARITY BALL

Budget carefully so that the décor and entertainment are done right without taking away too much from the charitable funds.

Engage a band or other music option that makes dancing irresistible and contagious but that doesn't detract from the focus of the event.

For out-of-town events, give guests favors that make memorable souvenirs of the venue and event but that are also helpful during their stay.

Even if you are hosting your own portion of a larger event, add individual touches to personalize and make guests feel important.

COVERT OPERATION

WHO: Gene Jones, "Mrs. Dallas Cowboys"

WHAT: A very special secret mission

WHEN: Husband Jerry's 60th birthday

WHERE: The Jones headquarters

WHY: "You only live once"

MIXING ELEMENTS FROM SEVERAL classic Bond movies, the video invitation began like this: "The following message is classified and its contents are top secret. This is priority one . . . and this is for your eyes only." (Can't you just hear that unforgettable James Bond theme music?) The subject: Jerry Jones. The mission: you only live once.

Between clips of Bond movies and that signature theme song, the video gave the details for the 007-themed surprise birthday party that Gene Jones masterfully plotted for her husband, Jerry, legendary owner of

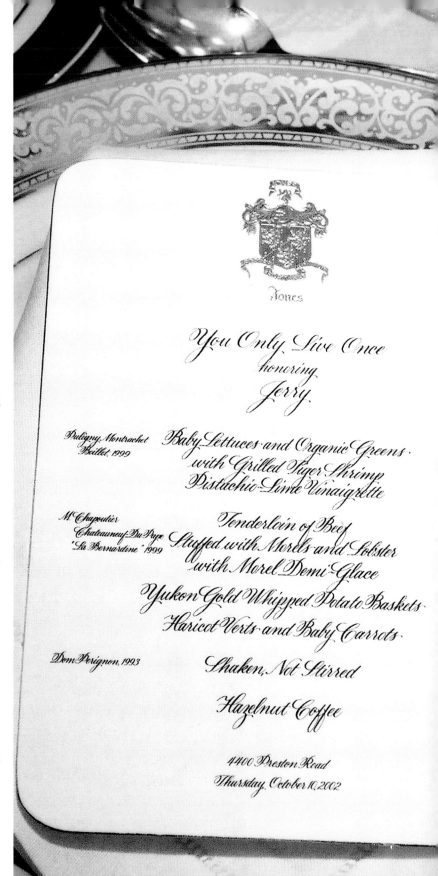

The inspiration for the memorable theme was the guest of honor himself.

the Dallas Cowboys football team. The attire was "black tie, gold, and *Diamonds Are Forever*." The location: Gene and Jerry's spacious manse in Dallas. The video concluded with the fitting *Mission Impossible* script, "This message will self-destruct in five seconds."

Even the packaging was brilliant. Special video jacket covers resembled a James Bond movie rental. They were sent in gold envelopes labeled *"For Your Eyes Only."*

The inspiration for the memorable theme was the guest of honor himself. "I wanted something appropriate for Jerry and that reminded me of him," Gene explained. "Since James Bond movies were his favorites through the years, this was an easy and obvious choice"—not to mention the fact that some might describe Jerry's mythical persona and jet-setting lifestyle as somewhat Bond-like.

Slipping into the world of secret agents for the evening, guests were first greeted by security and valets dressed in black suits and dark glasses. Jaws, the metal-mouthed bad

The drama heightened as a Bond impersonator and his girls took center stage

guy in many of the earlier Bond movies, was resurrected to serve as a doorman. "I always like something very special outside my front door," Gene mused. Just inside the door, Gene received the guests, and then "Bond girls" guided them to the terrace for cocktails and hors d'oeuvres. The Bond girls wore va-va-voom dresses hand-selected by the hostess, while the servers wore white jackets and dark shades. Also on the terrace was a one-of-a-kind martini bar—the vodka was poured through a 007 ice sculpture. A jazz band was the first of several music ensembles.

After Jerry arrived and the surprise was unveiled, Bond theme music filled the air and fog machines added to the drama. As the Bond girls fell in line down the terrace steps, a Sean Connery impersonator appeared and announced, "Bond, James Bond . . . Were you expecting someone else?" This was the not-so-subtle cue

for the guests to move outside to the tent to be seated for dinner.

Because the Joneses entertain so frequently, they had a custom tent constructed for their larger gatherings. It was designed to match the architecture of their residence and can be installed as needed in their grand backyard. "I love the clear tent in the setting of our garden," Gene explains. "You can see the beautiful tall trees and the flowers . . . it seems as if you're sitting outside in our garden, yet you're protected from the rain, which has definitely challenged us many times!"

Instead of numbering dinner tables for seating assignments, they were distinguished by popular Bond movie titles. And for tabletop décor, Gene decided on an elegant yet masculine ambiance. Centerpieces consisted of acrylic plateaus topped with orchids, large quartz crystal pieces, and votive candles. On alternating tables, tall vases filled with faux rock crystals sprayed stunning white orchids. In order to give events such as this a personal touch, the Jones

A progressive series of entertainers kept partygoers, as well as the birthday boy, captivated.

family crest is embossed on the menu cards and linens. Cocktail and dinner napkins are embroidered with their classic monogram.

The entertainment began with Bond movie clips featured on a screen over the tent's stage, and on side screens, shadow dancers reenacted the slinky moves seen in the big-screen preludes. All this while an eighteen-piece orchestra belted out the movie theme songs. The next act, French action painter Jean François, engaged the guests as the stage was prepared for the main attraction. His high-energy performance consisted of a splatter-painting technique choreographed to music with a lot of charismatic French dialogue thrown in. Although he seems to haphazardly "splatter" paint on a 12 x 12-foot canvas, his routine culminates as he turns the canvas upside down to reveal an incredible portrait of the guest of honor.

In perhaps the best-kept secret of the

evening, Gladys Knight arrived onstage and stole the show with a sensational performance tailored to include many of Jerry's favorite songs and the James Bond theme song that she recorded years ago. Finally, an upbeat dance band performed, and revelers took to the dance floor to join the action. "Jerry loves great music. He always has so much input on the music we have for parties. Because of the surprise, I was under extra pressure since I couldn't discuss it with him," Gene said. "I knew we wanted a very special entertainer—one whose music we had enjoyed through the years."

While the guests were dominating the dance

TIPS FOR KEEPING UP WITH THE JONESES

When you create a theme, follow it throughout all aspects of the event.

Costumed servers are a creative continuation of the party theme.

If you entertain often, maintain some consistency in your events that becomes your trademark, such as using monogrammed napkins.

Sending guests photos from the event is always an appreciated gesture and can serve as a post-party favor.

Changing the style of music during the course of the evening can signal a change in activity or mood.

Every detail matters if you want your party to be memorable.

floor, the valets strategically placed autographed Gladys Knight compact discs in their cars. They were packaged in gold envelopes stating "Mission Complete." "A lot of thought always goes in to the party favors. Everyone loves a memento from the party," Gene said. In addition, photos from the evening were later mailed to the guests in special monogrammed portmanteau.

"I take great care with every detail, from linens to crystal to flowers," Gene states emphatically. "It's very important to me. I am personally involved in each minor detail of every party. I want it to be memorable." And, after all, Jerry only turns sixty once.

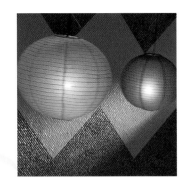

NEW YEAR'S EVE AT THE MARITIME

WHO: Marc Biron and Anthony Coppers

WHAT: Event planning European-style

WHEN: New Year's Eve

WHERE: New York's Maritime Hotel

WHY: "Socializing is a necessity"

SOMETIMES A DAY JOB is also a night job, and sometimes it's an all-night job. Such is the case with Marc Biron and Anthony Coppers, a European duo who have been effectively raising the pulse on New York's party circuit and redesigning the way New Yorkers let their hair down. In fact, they've made a career of it. Their company, Biron Coppers Communications Group, specializes in public relations, event planning, and product placement. It gives these popular young men-about-town an excuse to entertain a phenomenal six to twenty times a month!

> "Always find something new
> to make your guests have
> a special feeling or emotion—
> a dance, a light effect,
> musical instruments.

As New York's latest rulers of the night, Biron and Coppers have successfully captured the attention of the city's newest class of party revelers—an international collection of bright young things. An indication that these guys truly have a corner on this market: when they organized an event for the most anticipated night of the party calendar year—New Year's Eve—more than 2,000 guests turned out.

The site of this bash was the just-completed Maritime Hotel. "Bringing a new location to New Yorkers is always a good way to attract them," Coppers advises. "We were entertaining a crowd that was getting bored with a city offering too much at the same time." But even if you don't have a new location in which to entertain, Coppers stresses the importance of presenting other novelties in order to ensure the success of events. "Always find something new to make your guests have a special feeling or emotion—a dance, a light effect, musical instruments. It's not your event—it's theirs."

As for the New Year's Eve extravaganza, it was the lighting, the entertainment, and the hotel's own design that fused together to cre-

ate the type of fantasy party that typifies the essence that is New Year's Eve. The Maritime Hotel offered the perfect backdrop for the occasion. It is finished in dark nautical hues, an attractive mix of metal and wood

décor, curved ceilings, and a stunning mezzanine. Particularly mesmerizing are the surreal blue lighting and displays of mosaic tile. Colored-paper globe lights draped from the ceiling added to the underground nightclub's atmosphere.

After being awed by the new setting and innovative design, guests were treated to an old favorite—a band that seems to appeal to every taste, The Gypsy Kings. In those moments

TIPS FOR PLANNING A EURO-STYLE EVENT

It's not about you. Every element of the event should be for the benefit the guests.

Give them something new, whether it's a location, entertainment, lighting, etc.

Don't let the entertainment end too early—a late night is often the best kind.

Give your guests a sensory experience. Focus on creating feelings and emotions.

Broadcast your event on the Web for would-be attendees.

when the band wasn't performing its timeless, lively tunes, three different DJs took the musical reins. Biron and Coppers believe that attendees should have a total sensory experience, so they added fire-eaters, sword swallowers, and stilt walkers to perform throughout the night. One guest described the whole scene as "edgy and intensely passionate."

One of Coppers' philosophies of event organization is to "put yourself in the skin of your guests. As Europeans we have a different way of seeing event planning," he explains. "We want to make sure that every guest feels comfortable from the moment they come in, to the moment they leave . . . doormen, music, entertainment, bars, coat check, lights, tables. Everything is important." At this event they even catered to would-be guests who had to miss the action—the whole event was broadcast live via Web cast.

Of course, there was the traditional champagne toast at midnight, but in typical European style, that's when Biron and Coppers' events are just getting warmed up. At their parties you won't see the band pack up at 1 a.m., and most of the guests happily oblige the invitation to stay all night.

A HOSTESS FOR ALL SEASONS

WHO: Kelly Green, year-round hostess

WHAT: Lunching with girlfriends

WHEN: A lovely spring afternoon

WHERE: The grand salon in the Greens' Dallas home

WHY: Entertaining is one of life's great joys

"IF YOU LOVE TO ENTERTAIN, you should just do it, in any way that you can." Such is the advice of quintessential hostess Kelly Green. And for those hostesses who, despite their love of company, panic at the thought of having guests over for a seated dinner, Kelly prescribes a surprising antidote: entertain more often. "Entertaining twice a year is much more work than entertaining all the time," she expounds. It is her philosophy that a hostess should do the honors abundantly until she is comfortable enjoying herself instead of losing herself in the details of the party. "If you are

Hostess Kelly Green thinks about the food and wine before any other element of the party.

nervous, the guests will pick up on that," she explains.

Flexibility is one of her key ingredients to a successful soiree. She advocates having a definite plan while being able to make changes midstream when necessary. This may mean simply switching from a buffet-style setup to serving guests the dessert course at their tables if they seem inclined to remain seated. And, then, there are the more dramatic situations. Years ago Kelly and her husband, Norman, hosted a party outdoors in the country. Suddenly the wind changed and sent a mini tornado their way. "We just carried on and enjoyed it, although everything was blown apart," she laughs. Not just any hostess could take that scenario in stride, but when you entertain as often as Kelly does, experience just takes over. And such mishaps certainly make for good conversation!

Kelly's expertise in the art of entertaining first developed by way of her French upbringing. "While I was growing up in Canada, my family traditionally entertained on Sunday evenings. It was very much about the food

and the wine. We had small plates of food, but we could talk about what was on the plate for two hours," she reminisces. Now, at her own frequent fetes, the focus on culinary delights still prevails. "I am a foodie," she declares. "I think about the food and wine before anything else."

Entertaining in the Greens' homes—whether it's their summerhouse in the mountains of Canada or their home base in Dallas—is inspired by the seasons. Kelly has favorite menus as well as preferred rooms, depending on the time of year. In the fall and winter she favors the kitchen, and wild game is often the main course. Summer is perfect for grilling outside in Canada and dining under the stars next to the outdoor fireplace. Springtime in Dallas brings beautiful light into her grand salon, where lamb with vegetables is a common entrée.

This particular spring afternoon,
Kelly selected the grand salon setting to host six girlfriends for lunch.
The room is a re-creation of a
Parisian home with antique pieces
imported by the home's previous
owner. Also from France are Kelly's
eighteenth-century glasses, which
add to the historic romance of the
setting. On the menu is West Indies
Avocado Soup, Warm Maine
Lobster Asparagus Crepes, and
Lemon Napoleon—all as divine as
the luxurious surroundings.

Kelly reveals that creating invitations is one of her favorite parts of
entertaining, so she mails invites no
matter how small or informal the
gathering may be—even if she's
merely having six people in the
kitchen, which is one of her favorite
ways to entertain. They may be
handwritten or printed, but she
believes they should always invoke
the feeling of the gathering. The

TIPS FOR THOUGHTFUL HOSTING

Entertain often. The more you do it, the easier it becomes.

You know what they say about "the best laid plans"—be ready to make changes when necessary without drawing attention.

Make the hostess job easier by preparing crystal and linen ahead.

Don't be afraid to ask guests to perform tasks, such as keeping glasses filled. Most guests enjoy participating.

Send an invitation no matter how small the gathering. Guests will appreciate the effort.

invitation for this luncheon was decorated with a single flower.

Flowers play an important role in Kelly's entertaining. She works with Chris Whanger of J & C Design in Dallas to achieve a contemporary style much like the designs found at the Georges V hotel in Paris. "I like to keep the flowers simple against the formal backdrop of the house," she says. And in regard to the single stems floating in the stacked square vases for this occasion, she explains, "With one flower floating in each vase, the flower really has a face to it." She

continues, "They are also beautiful at night with candles behind them." But flowers on the table are not always a must-have. Sometimes guests will find vegetables cleverly arranged in crystal bowls.

In order to make the role of hostess a bit easier, Kelly advises having crystal and linen clean and ready to use. "These are a real nuisance to be dealing with the day of the party and are more easily dealt with on a puttering kind of Saturday," she suggests. On the day of the event, she leaves a couple of hours free for finishing touches—whether it's the table, the menu, or the room in general. "Quiet time to enjoy the anticipation of a gathering should be every hostess's gift to herself."

RECIPES BY GEORGE BROWN FOR THE KELLY GREEN LUNCHEON

WEST INDIES AVOCADO SOUP
Makes 8 servings

2 avocados, ripe
4 cups chicken stock
2 cups half-and-half
4 tablespoons white rum
1 1/2 teaspoons curry powder
1 teaspoon kosher salt
2 limes, juiced
1 lime, sliced into wheels
crème fraiche, optional

Peel the avocado and cut into pieces. In a blender, combine avocado, stock, cream, rum, curry powder, salt, and lime juice and blend until smooth and creamy. Chill for one hour. To serve, pour 6 ounces (about a cup) into a cold soup bowl and garnish with a lime wheel. Crème fraiche is also a nice complement to this soup. Drizzle it over top for a variation.

Warm Maine Lobster Asparagus Crepes with Sun-dried Tomato Salad and Champagne Vinaigrette
Makes 8 servings

For the Lobster Asparagus:
3 Maine lobsters
1 bunch asparagus
1 pound spinach
1 teaspoon minced garlic
1 teaspoon minced shallots
2 tablespoons olive oil
6 ounces boursin cheese
1 tablespoon shaved fresh chives
1 tablespoon chopped fresh basil
1 lemon, zested
Kosher salt, to taste
Fresh-cracked black pepper, to taste

Preheat the grill. Blanch lobster in seasoned boiling water; cool in ice. Remove from shell and cut in a medium dice. Set aside.

Next cut the asparagus root ends off. Season with oil, salt and pepper, then cook on a hot grill. Cool and then slice on the bias. Set aside.

After washing spinach, remove stems and saute in a frying pan with garlic, shallots, and olive oil. Cool, then chop.

In a large mixing bowl, add prepared lobster, asparagus, and spinach. Mix in boursin, chives, basil, and lemon zest; season with salt and pepper. Gently fold together, don't over-mix. Set aside and prepare crepes.

For the crepes:
3 eggs
1¼ cups milk
2 tablespoons butter, melted
½ cup flour
½ teaspoon kosher salt
2 tablespoons shaved fresh chives
Cooking spray, as needed

Combine all ingredients except chives in a blender and mix until smooth. Stir in the chives with a spoon. Heat a crepe pan over medium-high heat. Ladle about 3 tablespoons of batter into the pan and tip and swirl so the batter runs to the edges. Cook the crepe until the batter solidifies, then flip and cook it until golden brown. Repeat until all the batter is used up. You will need 16 crepes.

Spread crepes out on a clean surface and divide lobster mix evenly onto the 16 crepes. Roll the crepes and place them on a cookie sheet that has been sprayed with cooking spray. Set aside.

For the salad with sun-dried tomatoes:
16 cherry or grape tomatoes, red or yellow, halved
1 teaspoon olive oil
Kosher salt, to taste
Fresh-cracked black pepper, to taste
1 pound micro greens, cleaned and dry

In a mixing bowl, lightly toss the tomatoes with the olive oil and salt and pepper, just coating them. Arrange the tomatoes on a wire rack and place a cookie sheet underneath.

Place in the oven at 150 degrees and leave for 4–6 hours. Check periodically after 4 hours, as they should not be dried to a crisp. Once dried and cooled, toss with greens and set aside.

For the Champagne Vinaigrette:
3 tablespoons canola oil
3 tablespoons extra virgin olive oil
3 tablespoons olive oil
5 tablespoons champagne vinegar
1 tablespoon minced garlic
½ tablespoon minced shallots
1 teaspoon Worcestershire sauce
1 teaspoon chopped fresh basil
½ teaspoon chopped fresh chives
½ teaspoon chopped fresh parsley
½ teaspoon chopped fresh oregano
1 lemon, juiced and zested
½ teaspoon fresh-cracked black pepper
Kosher salt, to taste

In a mixing bowl, whisk together oils. Then whisk in the champagne vinegar. Whisk in remaining ingredients. Best if made a day in advance.

To assemble crepes and salad:
Preheat oven to 350 degrees. Place the crepes in oven and heat 7–10 minutes, or until hot. While the crepes are heating, toss the Champagne Vinaigrette and Sun-dried Tomato Salad in a mixing bowl. When crepes are hot, place two on a plate, side by side. Using tongs, put a small bunch of salad on top of the crepes. Serve immediately.

Lemon Napoleon with Fresh Fruit
Makes 12 servings

For the Napoleon:
3 sheets puff pastry
Flour

Lightly flour countertop and lay pastry sheets flat. With a rolling pin, roll each pastry out to ⅛ inch thick and trim edges neatly. Line three cookie sheets with parchment paper, then place a rolled-out pastry on each. Place another piece of parchment paper over top of each pastry, then put another cookie sheet on top of each parchment paper. If your cookie sheets are not very heavy, it may be necessary to place some weights on the top cookie sheet. (This will allow the pastry sheets to bake flat and evenly.)

Place in a 350-degree convection oven, or a 400 degree conventional oven, and bake 30–40 minutes, or until the pastry is deep golden brown, crisp, and baked through completely. Remove from oven, take off the cookie sheet, and allow to cool completely.

For the lemon filling:
1 cup lemon juice, freshly squeezed
1¼ cups butter
1¾ cups sugar
5 eggs
½ cup egg yolks
¾ teaspoon cornstarch

Place the lemon juice, butter, and sugar in a saucepan. Slowly bring to a boil. Combine eggs, yolks, and cornstarch in a mixing bowl and whisk. Just before the lemon juice starts to boil, ladle out 1 cup and pour over egg mixture. Whisk quickly. Once the lemon juice has reached the boiling point, pour egg mixture into the saucepan. Whisk quickly and constantly until the mixture thickens. Pour mixture into a flat casserole dish and allow to cool, but stir often. When the lemon mixture reaches room temperature, place a piece of plastic wrap directly onto its surface. Chill in the refrigerator.

For the fruit:
2 cups raspberry sauce
1 cup powdered sugar, in a shaker
2 cups raspberries
2 cups blackberries
2 cups strawberries, quartered
12 mint leaf tips

To assemble:
Place one sheet of pastry on a flat cutting board the same size or larger than the pastry. Spread about 1 cup of lemon filling evenly over the surface. Place the next sheet of pastry on top, and then spread the remaining lemon filling over top. Place the last sheet of pastry on top of that. Press down gently to compress.

Cut the napoleon with a sharp serrated knife into twelve equal-sized rectangles. Drizzle raspberry sauce over twelve dessert plates, then gently place napoleon rectangles over top. Generously sprinkle with powdered sugar and arrange berries next to napoleon. Garnish with a mint tip and serve.

PRESIDENTIAL PROTOCOL

WHO: Sam and Charles Wyly, founders of the Ranger Capital Group

WHAT: Black-tie investor dinner featuring former president George H. W. Bush

WHEN: On the occasion of a business meeting

WHERE: The Adolphus Hotel, Dallas, Texas

WHY: Rolling out the red carpet for the inaugural event

WHEN SAM AND CHARLES WYLY began envisioning an inaugural event for what would become an annual business meeting for the prestigious investment management company they founded, Ranger Capital Group, they didn't want just any other corporate dinner. It had to be memorable, first class, a statement. It had to be far from "corporate." After all, the investors are the types who have done everything and been everywhere, and not just any dinner would

The historic Adolphus
Hotel was chosen for its
regal and aristocratic flair.

persuade them to clear their hectic schedules for a trip to Dallas.

Susan Tiholiz, who helped coordinate the event for Ranger Capital, explained that the extravagant affair for 400 guests was also to reflect the values of the relatively new company to its investors. "Our desire was to express Ranger Capital as extremely service oriented, warm, and welcoming," Tiholiz said. "Corporate events can sometimes feel cold and stiff," she pointed out, "and this was to be more of a social gathering wrapped around a business event."

The first invitation extended was to the guest speaker, former president George Herbert Walker Bush. His presence alone guaranteed that the evening would be unique. Event consultant Sally Jones was then enlisted to make sure the rest of the evening's details were sufficiently grandiose.

The historic Adolphus Hotel was chosen for its regal and aristocratic flair. Since its doors opened in 1912, many presidents and members of royalty have chosen to stay at this elegant Dallas landmark. The hotel looks regal with its Renaissance-inspired ceiling murals in the

RANGER CAPITAL GROUP

REQUESTS THE PLEASURE OF YOUR COMPANY

FOR A PRIVATE DINNER

WITH REMARKS FROM

The Honorable George Herbert Walker Bush

THURSDAY, THE SEVENTH OF NOVEMBER

COCKTAILS AND VIEWING OF "ROSIE THE RIVETER"

AT HALF AFTER SIX O'CLOCK

DINNER AT HALF AFTER SEVEN O'CLOCK

THE ADOLPHUS HOTEL

DALLAS, TEXAS

BLACK TIE

The exquisitely calligraphed invitation signaled that this was an event not to be missed.

ballrooms, which are quite magnificent even without a single flower or shred of added décor. The location was therefore perfect for this event: it naturally invoked a sense of tradition and trust. "The Adolphus really rolled out the red carpet," Jones said, "which is, of course, what they are known for."

Stately invitations announcing the black-tie gala were luxurious ivory-embossed cards printed in gray. The exquisite calligraphy further signaled the exceptional climate of the evening. Guests knew upon receipt that this was an event not to be missed.

When the evening finally arrived, guests were treated not only to some cocktails and

"It seemed like a party
that could have been at
the White House."

hors d'oeuvres as a string quartet entertained, but also to a viewing of Norman
Rockwell's famed painting *Rosie the
Riveter,* which had recently been purchased by Ranger Endowment. The painting, which was created for the cover of
the May 29, 1943, *Saturday Evening Post,*
gave visual form to the millions of
American women who answered the government's call to enter the workforce and
fill traditionally male jobs left vacant by
those who had gone to fight in WW II.
This jewel of American history, along
with the speech by former president
George H. W. Bush, whose own heroic
service in WW II is well known, added a
patriotic flavor to the event.

Inside the ballroom, rich colors embel-
lished the already majestic setting. Dinner
tables were draped in gold or green embroidered linens. Jewel-toned china, specially
brought in from California, was paired with

*One guest declared this was the most beautiful party
she had ever attended.*

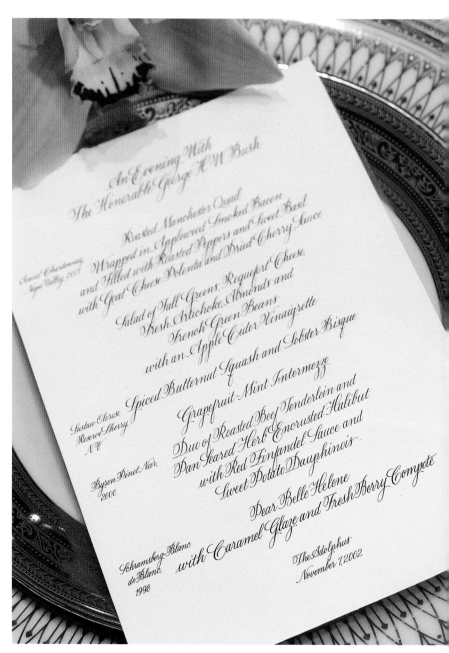

TIPS FOR
MIXING
BUSINESS
WITH
PLEASURE

Business events do not need to feel "corporate." Create a warm social atmosphere even when there are necessary business undertones.

Decide on an image or qualities you wish to convey about your company and build your event around them.

When looking to go the extra mile, commission calligraphy to add elegance to invitations and menu cards.

Invite a unique keynote speaker to ensure a large and enthusiastic turnout.

glassware trimmed in gold. Local florist The Garden Gate created vibrant floral arrangements that captured the formality and flamboyance of the occasion. As a final touch, each place setting was decorated with a splendid single orchid.

While the Honorable George H. W. Bush gave personal remarks regarding the family's father and son presidencies, and humorous stories from the Bush family archives, guests were served a six-course feast fit for kings. Masterfully created by chef William Koval, the first course consisted of roasted quail wrapped in apple-wood-smoked bacon and filled with roasted peppers, and sweet basil with goat cheese and dried cherry sauce. Next was a salad of fall greens, Roquefort cheese,

fresh artichoke, almonds, and French-style green beans with an apple cider vinaigrette. Then spiced butternut squash and lobster bisque. Before the main course: grapefruit mint intermezzo. On to the roasted beef tenderloin and pan-seared encrusted halibut with red Zinfandel sauce and sweet potato *dauphinois*. The finale was the pear belle Helene with caramel glaze and fresh berry compote. All were divine.

After the event concluded, one high-profile guest, the wife of a former governor, declared it the most beautiful party she had ever attended. And Sally Jones had her own take on the formal affair. "It seemed like a party that could have been at the White House."

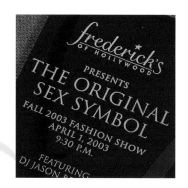

WHAT LIES BENEATH

WHO: Frederick's of Hollywood

WHAT: Fashion show and auction

WHEN: Los Angeles Fashion Week

WHERE: Smashbox Studios, Culver City, California

WHY: A benefit for breast cancer research

DESPITE THE NONSTOP PARTY that is Hollywood, not many charity events can provoke celebrities to show off their undergarments. But that's exactly what happened when Frederick's of Hollywood hosted an auction to benefit breast cancer research. The coveted item chosen to solicit bids was—what else?—celebrity-designed bras. Sixty of Tinseltown's hottest stars were each given a basic black Frederick's bra with which to create their own one-of-a-kind lot for the auction. And as everyone who attended the festivities found out, underwear can really make an impact—in more ways than one.

SHERYL CROW

Celebrities including Jennifer Aniston, Cindy Crawford, and Sharon Stone created one-of-a-kind bras for the auction.

This spirited soiree called for a sexy yet innovative invitation. The hosts' well-suited solution was see-through pieces of red Lucite printed with gold lettering announcing the Frederick's of Hollywood "The Original Sex Symbol" Fashion Show and accompanying auction. A curvy "F" for Frederick's was shaded into the pseudo-glass, and a matching cutout of the letter on the invitation's red sleeve made for an alluring first impression.

Creating the appropriate décor for the event had its own challenges. Add an assembly of big-name Hollywood actors with a slew of catwalking models scantily clad in lingerie, and it is an accomplishment in itself if partygoers even notice what color the room is. But the swanky scene in the tent outside of Smashbox Studios was undeniably eye-catching with its red hues and mix of modern shapes. Guests lounged on red couches under

palm trees. They mingled at cocktail tables draped in red velvet and topped with clear glass votives. Funky red light fixtures made psychedelic designs on the floor, and the Fredericks of Hollywood logo was projected onto the backdrop of the tent.

Treats for the guests also blended with the color scheme, including bottles of Perrier and color-coordinated green Perrier lollypops that were passed on

TIPS FOR AN INTIMATE AFFAIR

When creating invitations, think outside the box. Paper is not a requirement.

Adding sex appeal to an event, as with most things in life, makes it more enticing.

Always have an open bar and plenty of specialty drinks when hosting a charity auction.

Seduce your guests with atmosphere and music.

Try to attract celebrity participation instead of just appearances.

square acrylic trays. A full bar with special red and green martinis helped to loosen up the guests, as well as their checkbooks.

The bras themselves were the real conversation pieces of the evening. Displayed on red Lucite tables, they doubled as fantastic decorations. Susan Sarandon and daughter Eva Amurri created a bra featuring images of Jim Morrison adorning each cup. Sheryl Crow's creation was covered in hundreds of hot-pink guitar picks. Sharon Stone chose to include feather butterflies in her design, while Cindy Crawford selected a motif of black sequins and red lips. Jennifer Aniston's contribution showed off a pair of strategically placed hands. The men had equal opportunity to create: Ed Harris also chose a "hands-on" theme, using two leather mitts, and Garry Shandling made his out of two large royal blue yarmulkes that he quipped could be called a "bramulke."

After an introductory speech by chairperson actress Tea Leoni, actor Kevin Nealon emceed the event. Only six of the clever creations were sold to the party guests via live auction. Celebrity guests modeled the lots over their clothes, simultaneously seducing guests and raising the bids. Julianne Moore's design of blue and white bugle beads fetched $9,000. By the end of the evening, $40,000 had been raised for Expedition Inspiration Take-A-Hike to fund breast cancer research at the UCLA Jonsson and USC Norris Cancer centers. But that was just the beginning of the fundraising. The remaining garments were put on Internet display at sothebys.com for anyone to bid on.

In addition to aiding a very worthy cause, a secondary effect of the live auction of intimates was uncovered: "I feel unbelievably sexy," a pregnant Brooke Shields told the crowd about the bras. "As an expectant mother, you feel like you are going to lose your sex appeal, but not with these."

NEW YORK'S YELLOW ROSE OF TEXAS

WHO: New York's leading ladies

WHAT: Liz Smith's 80th birthday bash

WHEN: February 2, now Liz Smith Day

WHERE: Le Cirque, New York City

WHY: The perfect party for the ultimate partygoer

WHEN EIGHT HIGH-PROFILE FRIENDS of famous gossip columnist Liz Smith joined forces to give her an eightieth birthday party, there was no question that it had to be a first-class event. The nationally syndicated journalist attends nearly every major party in New York, as she has done for decades, and is often the one entertaining while simultaneously digging up scoop for her six-days-a-week column. In other words, Liz Smith is a woman who loves a great party. And these eight hostesses know how to throw one. All power

A COMMEMORATIVE POSTCARD
ON THE OCCASION OF
QUEEN LIZ'S 80TH BIRTHDAY,
FEBRUARY 2ND, 2003

"GOSSIP IS NEWS RUNNING AHEAD OF ITSELF IN A RED SILK DRESS."—LIZ SMITH

players in New York society and leading ladies in their respective industries, these women didn't ascend to their lofty positions by doing things in an ordinary way. The team included literary agent Joni Evans, producer and correspondent Cynthia McFadden, Barbara Walters, former Texas governor Ann Richards, *Good Housekeeping*'s Ellen Levine, philanthropist Louise Grunwald, television producer Joan Ganz Cooney, and writer Marie Brenner.

For this prestigious group, planning the perfect party for the ultimate partygoer was carried out in their usual fashion—with flawless attention to detail. For four months prior to the party, they met once a month at Michael's restaurant in Manhattan for breakfast and planning. They e-mailed, they phoned, they faxed. "It was like a summit," Joni Evans said. "We considered everything."

The first order of business was compiling the guest list. Just like a Liz Smith column, it included a collection of stars worthy of bold-face type: Mr. and Mrs. Oscar de la Renta,

Diane Von Furstenberg, Walter Kronkite, Peter Jennings, Diane Sawyer, Mayor Mike Bloomberg, and on and on. The honor of presenting toasts to the birthday girl was given to four of Liz's favorite men: Pete Peterson of Blackstone Financial, director Joel Schumacher, director Mike Nichols, and famed Democrat Vernon Jordan.

With such a star-studded cast, the next consideration was a stage worthy to serve as a backdrop for the festivities. After reflecting on many venues, the ladies chose Le Cirque, a restaurant so frequently attended by the guest of honor

that it would make a most comfortable fit.

A design was then created for the invitation that depicted Liz looking at her Madame Tussaud's wax figure counterpart and invited guests to celebrate "the real Mary Elizabeth." The one person who did not receive the invitation was Liz herself. "I knew that my friends were giving me a party, but I didn't know which of my friends. Nobody would tell me anything," Liz explained. "They just said, 'Get dressed up and Joel Schumacher is going to pick you up.' I only had to show up and be eighty years old," she said.

When she did arrive at Le Cirque, she

found that the hostesses had selected a Yellow Rose of Texas theme to reflect Liz's Fort Worth roots. "When people walk into the room they should feel comfortable, the room should be welcoming and beautiful," Ellen Levine advises. "Especially for a personal celebratory event like a birthday party, the room should not be overwhelming. The party is about the person you are celebrating, not about the décor."

In celebration of the birthday girl, all the ladies received yellow boas and the men were given yellow rose boutonnieres. These festive accessories were arranged in sterling bowls next to a framed *Vanity Fair* cover featuring Liz. In the dining room, Liz's friend Gayford Steinberg had created beautiful yellow rose centerpieces in silver vases set atop tables draped in luxurious brown velvet. Votive holders covered in yellow rose petals lit up the room. Even the birthday cake, in the shape of a typewriter, was adorned with edible yellow roses.

Following cocktails, the guests were treated to a seated dinner. At each place setting was a commemorative postcard of "Queen" Liz and her wax counterpart (which also made a debut at the party). Printed across the postcard was one of Liz's most memorable quotes, "Gossip is news running ahead of itself in a red silk dress."

Although there were Texas undertones, it was indeed a New York evening, so Mayor Bloomberg was chosen to start the festivities.

His first order of business was to designate February 2 as Liz Smith Day. Then, the other most notable Texan in the room, former Texas governor Ann Richards, emceed the evening with her famous twang and sharp tongue. The entertainment was arguably better than any Broadway show: Bette Midler, Liza Minnelli, Tommy Tune, and Michael Buble all serenaded the birthday girl, and Liz made her own contribution when she joined Liza to belt out a rendition of "New York, New York."

"I was quite stunned that these women had gotten together and done all of this behind my back," Liz said. "It was just wonderful. I had such a good time, despite the fact that, like most people, I hate surprises."

TIPS FOR A PARTY WORTHY OF THE GOSSIP COLUMNS

Give yourself enough planning time for sorting out all the details without any rush.

For birthday celebrations, make sure the decorations are not overwhelming. The party is about the guest of honor, not the décor.

Enlist specific guests in advance to make toasts to the honoree. Even the most articulate of speakers will do better if given an opportunity to prepare.

Even if the party is not a complete surprise, try to dazzle the guest with surprise personal touches and tributes.

PRETTY IN PASTELS

WHO: Alice + Olivia, Lacoste, and MAC cosmetics

WHAT: "Pretty in Pastels"

WHEN: Springtime in Manhattan

WHERE: Cipriani Sutton Lounge

WHY: Launch party for Alice + Olivia denim

WHILE ANYONE CAN GO OUT and buy a great pair of jeans or a fabulous top, it's those who have an eye for artfully tying together the various pieces of an outfit who truly achieve great style. There are a lot of fashion folk in Manhattan—editors, stylists, socialites, models, celebrities—who are known for this talent. It was to these types that Stacey Bendet Weiner, designer of the hip Alice + Olivia clothing line, wanted to introduce her new denim offerings. The best way to launch what will invariably become objects of desire, of course, is to have a party. In case you didn't catch this on *Sex*

Just like fashioning a great outfit, it's
the creative tying together of elements
that makes a party.

and the City—the one thing that New Yorkers like as much as clothes is parties.

The Alice + Olivia line did not include tops, so Weiner sought out a label that would complement the party *and* the outfits. That's where Lacoste came in. "Their polos are such a great fit with the jeans that we wanted to coordinate with them on the event," Weiner explains. Gigi Howard, public relations director of Lacoste, agrees: "Lacoste polos, in many different vibrant colors, are super fun, sexy, and chic with Alice + Olivia low-cut jeans." MAC cosmetics further complemented the ensemble with contributions of its sassy spring shades. Ultimately, what was a perfect fit for the jeans also made for an ideal party partnership.

Just like fashioning a great outfit, it's the creative tying together of elements that makes a party. After considering the colorful palette that their various products created, the hostesses gave their event a title and a theme—"Pretty in Pastels."

Cipriani Sutton proved the right venue for what the girls had in mind. "For the launch of the Alice + Oliva denim line, we wanted to do something glamorous and girly," Weiner said. "We chose Cipriani because the décor was feminine and pretty and this was a major theme of the party." The room itself, with its elegant couches and chaises, is already cozy and welcoming. But the hostesses added their own personal touches. Guests arrived to find the décor, naturally, done up in pretty pastels. Pink candies in silver bowls along with pale roses and votive candles decorated the tabletops and mantels. Images of made-up female faces were projected onto rotating discs that hung from the ceiling like ornaments. Perhaps most importantly, several mannequins displayed the stylish union of Lacoste shirts with Alice + Olivia denim.

Weiner explains that she favors quirky entertaining with a twist, "like having ballerinas in a fashion show or a musical performance at a cocktail party to make it special." So, to give this event a little of the unexpected, the hostesses hired Rene Risque and the Art Lovers

The party was a successful blending of fashion and entertainment—fun, funky, and smart.

(musicians with a comic slant) to entertain. This act has created quite a sensation with their satirical portrayal of rock stars, fashionistas, and the glam world of consumption, which all eternally overlap in existence. Rene himself wore a Lacoste shirt and low-slung Alice + Olivia pants, and as expected, poked fun at the likes of the fashionable hostesses and the beautiful people that filled the room. The show went over fabulously, and many guests took to the dance floor.

At the end of the evening, each guest received very personal party favors. Neatly packaged in pink-and-white bags were a pair of Alice + Olivia jeans, a Lacoste baby polo, and MAC make-up hand selected by the hosts for the particular guest's style and coloring (sizes were obtained in advance as part of the RSVP). Each guest also received a gift certificate for monogramming—so the jeans would make an even more personal fashion statement.

Further evidencing the parallels that exist between fashion and entertaining, Weiner's description of the Alice + Olivia look sounds a lot like that of the Pretty in Pastels party: "Fun (maybe a little quirky), funky (maybe a little retro), and smart (maybe a little fabulous too)." She's obviously one of those who can pull together an outfit or an event with great style.

TIPS FOR A TRENDSETTING DEBUT

Seek a co-host whose style complements yours.

Tie the elements of the party together creatively, like you would an outfit.

Unique and unexpected entertainment provides an unforgettable treat.

Giving extravagant, personal party favors is a sales technique that will continue selling long after the party is over.

HARVEST PARTY

WHO: Wine proprietors Kathryn and Craig Hall

WHAT: A weekend-long celebration

WHEN: The last full moon of the season

WHERE: In the hills of Napa Valley, California

WHY: Celebrating the end of the harvest

THE LAST FULL MOON OF HARVEST SEASON makes its appearance over the Napa Valley countryside, signaling the end of long hours of harvesting grapes and the beginning of long-awaited celebrations. It is a favorite time of year for Kathryn and Craig Hall, who annually host a weekend of seasonal festivities at their home and vineyard perched in the hills above Rutherford, California. The stunning settings alone—a modern hilltop house overlooking the wine country, and endless rows of grapes and flowers at the vineyard— make the parties wondrous experiences for the guests.

Celebrating the year's grape harvest is an annual event for the Halls. The festivities last the weekend and guests know the protocol in advance.

But as the weekend's events unfold in perfect synergy, it is obvious that the couple's talents extend far beyond the farming of fine grapes.

To say that the Halls are multi-talented is quite an understatement. Craig is a lifelong entrepreneur and author. In addition to his work at the Hall vineyards, he is involved in real estate and venture capital, technology, hotels, and international affairs. Kathryn grew up ensconced in her family's wine business, which she continued to oversee while becoming a successful attorney, business executive, community activist, and mother of two.

From 1997 to 2001, Kathryn served as the U.S. Ambassador to Austria. It was this position that she credits with having the greatest influence on her entertaining style. "There were receptions almost every day, and often more than one a day," she reminisces. That's when she learned the valuable reasons for fundamental protocol. "If people can expect a certain structure, it creates a comfort zone," she explains. "It is very important for people to feel comfortable."

Hence, the weekend celebration is always structured so guests can anticipate events and plan their schedules. The festivities begin on Friday with a casual welcome party at the vineyard. The late-afternoon timing allows

While at the vineyard, guests leisurely wander the sculpture-filled grounds, experience educational wine tastings, and enjoy an informal outdoor buffet.

out-of-town guests to settle in to their hotels prior to the party and then disperse afterwards to the area's many renowned restaurants. While at the vineyard, guests leisurely wander the sculpture-filled grounds, experience educational wine tastings, and enjoy an informal outdoor buffet. This year, tables were decorated in red hues (the color of the vineyard's wine labels), with autumn flora, vegetables, pumpkins, baskets, and even

stuffed roosters—all adding to the harvest motif.

Saturday evening brings the main attraction. One hour before sunset, guests arrive at the Hall home, where attendants promptly cater to their every need. "A party needs to be something special no matter what type of event it is. From the first moment, the guests should feel welcome," Kathryn says. To instantly create a jovial atmosphere, drinks are quickly in hand and flame throwers and dancers provide lively entertainment. The party's photographer lures each guest into a picture with the costumed performers, ensuring that everyone will receive at least one keepsake photograph from the event. Kathryn guarantees her own personal memories of the party by always providing a guest book, a habit she retains from her days at the embassy.

Recognizing that the flow of guests at a party is of great importance, Kathryn assigns precise roles to the party's staff and performers, who escort guests to the appropriate places at the necessary times. The first hour consists of wine, champagne, and passed hors d'oeuvres just outside of chez Hall. A jazz pianist provides the evening's first tunes while the sun makes its

"Give a party you'd like to go to yourself," is Kathryn Hall's advice. Several bands performed different styles of music, and dancing was the order of the evening.

dramatic descent into the cascading hills. As the full moon takes its post, guests are escorted down the hillside to the outdoor, seated dinner. "The full moon not only symbolizes the end of the harvest season, it also provides fantastic lighting for the outdoor event," Kathryn observes.

Napa is, of course, a place where expectations are high for exquisite food and wine and the ideal pairing of the two. So the Halls' grand buffet dinner always includes a large selection of well-thought-out local fare chosen to match the vintage selections of the evening. Tables again reflect the vineyard's red theme, with peppers and flowers mixed for bright centerpieces atop crisp white linens.

Another of Kathryn's philosophies is "to give a party you'd like to go to yourself." Since she personally has a penchant for dancing, she makes sure to engage bands that can accommodate. For this occasion, a swing-blues band performed during dinner, and later, guests danced off the Cabernet to rock-'n'-roll numbers under the stars.

Departing gifts to the guests were commemorative long-sleeve shirts that pictured the vineyard's unofficial logo—a sculpture of two metal figures toasting each other. The original commissioned work decorates the Halls' property, and the image appears on the vineyard's Web site, as well as on the invitation to the celebration weekend.

Although it may appear that the Halls have many interests, Kathryn says that the vineyard "is not one of our passions, it *is* our passion." Naturally, it is only fitting that their finely produced harvest party is as world-class as their wines.

TIPS FOR A HARVEST PARTY

When spreading activities over a weekend, be sure the guests know the schedule of events in advance.

The flow of people at the party should be as well planned as all of the other elements.

Take advantage of both the sunset and full moon to take your party from evening into night.

Commemorative photos make thoughtful keepsakes for guests.

Set out a guestbook to ensure your own memories of the party.

187

HILLSBORO HOUNDS HUNT CLUB

WHO: The Hillsboro Hounds Hunt Club

WHAT: A hunt tea

WHEN: At the conclusion of each hunt

WHERE: Nashville, Tennessee

WHY: Relaxation, recuperation, and plenty of horse talk

HENRY HOOKER, A LONG-STANDING MEMBER of the Hillsboro Hounds Hunt Club, described his first experience with the hunt in his book *Fox, Fin, and Feather:*

While I was courting her in 1955, Alice took me hunting for the first time. Mason Houghland and John Sloan Sr. made me very welcome. Vernon Sharp lent me a horse. The sky was emerald green, the horses full of run, hounds gaily and keen. I viewed a fox, which I still see in my fancy. That romance endures. The longer I hunt, the more I understand Mason Houghland's

The hunt club tea is fundamentally about the pleasure of each other's company.

advice: "The time to be happy is now, the place to be happy is here, the way to be happy is to hunt the fox."

From the earliest of times, people around the world have experienced similar affection for this exhilarating sport and the social interaction that thrives along with it. Hunt clubs have probably existed almost as long as hunts themselves, providing the foundations from which friendships, and no doubt many courtships, form.

In Tennessee, members of the Hillsboro Hounds Hunt Club, founded in 1932, have adopted the tradition of holding tea after each of their hunts. For them, every Wednesday and Saturday during the chilly hunt season brings a beloved day spent on horseback galloping through the great outdoors. Just before dark, about seventy-five members of the club ride over to the "hunt box" where the tea for that particular hunt is held.

Hunt boxes are cozy country residences that provide lodging for the hunters as well as their horses and hounds. Throughout the season, the club members take turns hosting the traditional

-painted hound used as a center-piece, a gift to the hunt club from a local artist who specializes in the carving of carrousel horses. This was the inaugural viewing of the hound carving for the club's members, and, along with the artist's attendance, it was a highlight of the event.

As is tradition at these teas, the club members relaxed and recuperated by the fire, took in a nourishing feast, and discussed the events of the day. Just like most gatherings in life, the hunt club tea is fundamentally about the pleasure of each other's company.

tea, which is actually more akin to a post-hunt dinner party than an actual tea. Hosts for this particular tea included Franklin, Tennessee, Mayor Dan Spears and his wife, Brenda, along with their friend Dale Wylie. It was held at the hunt box of Mr. and Mrs. Albert Menafee II. Just as you would expect at a traditional dinner party, the hosts put their own touches on the décor and on what is always a hearty buffet-style dinner.

For this tea, the hosts adorned their country tabletop with beautiful porcelain fox figurines atop a red-and-white-checked table covering. Also fitting for the occasion was the unique hand-carved and

TIPS FOR AN AFTER-SPORTS DINNER CLUB

If you belong to a seasonal sports club, take turns hosting the after-event meal.

Be sure the table is festively set even though you meet together often.

Allow time and places for relaxation and recuperating from the vigorous activity.

ACKNOWLEDGMENTS

THIS BOOK WOULD NOT HAVE BEEN POSSIBLE without the generous invitations and hospitality of the hosts who graciously included me in their events: Becca Cason Thrash; Maria Ignez Barbosa; Katherine, Elizabeth, and Melinda Mathes; Marci and Michael Warren; Joe and David Perry; Ken Downing and Sam Salidino; Jan Showers; Tricia Barnstable Brown; Gene Jones; Anthony Coppers and Marc Biron; Kelly Green; Sam Wyly; Gigi Howard and Stacey Bendet; Allison Hopkins and Skylar; Kathryn and Craig Hall; Margaret Hedberg; Brian Bolke; Mr. and Mrs. Albert Menafee; Joni Evans, Cynthia McFadden, Ann Richards, Ellen Levine, Louise Grunwald, Joan Ganz Cooney, Marie Brenner and Barbara Walters.

A special thank-you to those friends who kindly shared an introduction or an idea: Princess Michael of Kent, Barbara de Portago, Alan Kannof, Bethany Bultman, Doreen Nichols, Jerry Jones Jr., Sally Jones and Susan Tiholiz, Sheryl Dennis and Chopin Rabin, Stephen Pearce, Jocelyn White, Farris Rookstool III, Joey Fatone, Joe Mulvahill, Christophe Gollut, and Sheri and Summerlee Staten.

Thank you to the talented photographers whose work is featured: Mary Hilliard, Robert Bruno, Mali Azima, Kristina Bowman and Kristen and Stephen Karlisch. Thank you to Courtney Dreslin for reading my mind and putting what I was trying to say in the right words.

Thank you to the chefs who graciously shared their delicious recipes: Louise Kehnard, George Brown and James Rowland.

I am so grateful to have the support of so many friends and colleagues: Allison, Janet, Amy, Christy, Tim, Summerlee, Franklin and Gigi and the staff at RSVP—Soiree, Laurel, Katherine and Casey.

My dreams of writing this book came true thanks to the graciousness of Betty Lou Phillips and the guidance of Madge Baird.

Thank you to Trevor Erskine-Meade, Jan Miller, Jan Planit, Nicole Marra, Terri Thornton, Matthew Sanderson and Don Godwin for your assistance and advice.

Thank you to all of the Whitmans: I look forward to officially joining the Clan! A special thank you to Stuart and Caroline for your support and love. Big Kiss.

Thank you to my best friend, Justin, for your encouragement, advice and love. You make me so happy. I love you.

A most sincere thank you to my loving family—Kirby, Kari, Krystal, Big Mama and Daddy. I love you and always treasure the pleasure of your company.

WHAT   WHEN   WHERE   WHY   WHO   WHAT   WHEN   WHERE   WHY   WHO   V